ENTERTAINING

ENTERTAINING

MALCOLM
HILLIER

DK

DK PUBLISHING, INC.

A DK PUBLISHING BOOK

Visit us on the World Wide Web at
http://www.dk.com

PROJECT EDITOR Lesley Malkin
DESIGNER Murdo Culver
ASSISTANT DESIGNER Pauline Clarke
DTP DESIGNER Robert Campbell
PRODUCTION CONTROLLER Hélène Lamassoure
SENIOR MANAGING EDITOR Mary-Clare Jerram
MANAGING ART EDITOR Amanda Lunn
US EDITOR Laaren Brown

PHOTOGRAPHY Stephen Hayward
FOOD PHOTOGRAPHY Martin Brigdale
STYLIST Helen Trent
FOOD STYLISTS Janice Murfitt, Jane Suthering

First American Edition, 1997
2 4 6 8 10 9 7 5 3 1
Published in the United States by DK Publishing, Inc.
95 Madison Avenue, New York, New York, 10016

Library of Congress Cataloging-in-Publication Data

Hillier, Malcolm.
    Entertaining / by Malcolm Hillier
        p. cm.
    Includes index.
    ISBN 0–7894–1985–8
    1. Entertaining.   2. Menus.   3. Cookery.   I. Title.
TX731.H48 1997
642'.4—dc21   97–20569
                                                CIP

Text film output by R&B Creative Services,
Great Britain

Reproduced by Colourpath
Printed and bound in Great Britain by
Butler and Tanner Ltd, Frome and London

CONTENTS

INTRODUCTION 6

BREAKFAST & BRUNCH 26

LUNCH 44

RECIPE SYMBOL GUIDE

PREPARATION TIME   COOKING TIME
          OTHER TIME REQUIRED

HOSTING A

"Never eat more than you can lift." MISS PIGGY

THE FIRST STEP
I love the planning almost as much as the event: it is certainly all part of the fun that entertaining at home is supposed to be.

WHEN I WAS STILL STUDYING MUSIC, I became captivated by the idea of entertaining. To create a special time at home when people could appreciate each others' company and share some delicious food seemed the most exciting of prospects. A great friend and I used to vie with each other, as impoverished students, to produce the least expensive but most glamorous meal. Times have changed, but we have never looked back.

A lunch for two, a supper for six, a dinner for 12, or a buffet party for a crowd: I still think little beats the pleasure of entertaining a group of friends or family, enjoying food, drink, and lively conversation in your own home. Such events become milestones to anticipate, and then remember.

We all want the occasions on which we entertain to be a success. Although some effort is required to orchestrate any event so it proceeds smoothly with a minimum of worry, I find this effort is almost always richly rewarded. Remember also that the simplest of meals is frequently just as enjoyable as a more elaborate spread.

PARTY

Kitchen entertaining is what I enjoy most. Fortunately, my country kitchen in the middle of the city, with a large window overlooking the garden, is capacious enough for a table that will seat ten, leaving plenty of cooking space. The formal dining room down the hallway has been made into an office. I no longer feel isolated from guests while I prepare the food, and I believe my guests are much more relaxed about the whole dining experience, too.

Entertaining can be one of the great joys of life; it is one of mine. I have close friends who give an informal dinner party in their kitchen, every week, often for as many as twelve people. They say that it keeps them young, and to prove it they are still doing it in their mid-eighties. So send out the invitations, and prepare for you and your guests to enjoy yourselves.

DECIDING ON THE OCCASION

IDEAL PARTNERS
Always make sure that the food you serve suits the occasion and looks impressive with the table decorations you choose.

WHETHER THE DECISION TO ENTERTAIN springs from a simple desire to have a party, or you have some friends you would like to see, planning an event, in my mind, is as important as the event itself.

If it begins with the guests, how best to entertain them? Would they prefer a lazy lunch, an elegant dinner, a summer barbecue, or a refined tea? On the other hand, if your motivation is the occasion itself, you will need to decide on a guest list to suit the event. I always try to assemble a group that has at least one linking thread of interest and invite a good conversationalist. Also consider any restraints: how much time and expense can you spare? How much room (including oven and refrigerator space) do you have, and are you confident in catering to and entertaining large numbers?

TAKING CARE OF THE DETAILS

I find a party is easier to orchestrate if I plan it around a theme, perhaps dictated by the food I serve or the season: a vegetarian winter supper, an Italian buffet, or a summer barbecue. Plan the table setting and food presentation, remembering that small touches make all the difference.

COUNTRY HAMPER
PICNIC

FESTIVE CELEBRATION
DINNER

CHAMPAGNE
BUFFET

Entertaining is the very stuff of life

Inviting your guests can usually be done informally over the telephone. This often means an instant reply and gives you the opportunity to inquire about food dislikes or allergies. If you wish, send written invitations to make it more of an event. Remember to include a dress code, particularly if your theme requires it, as well as the reason for the party if it is a celebration.

WHAT FOOD TO SERVE

The key to a successful menu is balance: choose interesting ingredients, and consider how their flavors, colors, and textures interact with one another. Bear in mind that the freshest ingredients in season are always best. It is simple to mix and match the recipes given here, referring to the planning notes on each menu, as long as you always remember no two courses should be too rich. Never take on too much; it is vital that you are relaxed and at ease while you cook and entertain. Your guests will sense if you are not.

CONSIDER YOUR DRINKS

The type of occasion and the food you plan to serve are important considerations when deciding what to drink with your meal: a refined wine and fiery barbecue food will not do justice to each other. Serving an aperitif before the meal is a great way to relax your friends, but do make sure it is not so strong that it spoils the first course. A brandy, liqueur, or port with coffee after the meal is also welcome, especially in winter. When calculating how much wine to buy, I usually allow, on average, three glasses per person with the meal. Always stock up on mineral water and one soda alternative.

CHOOSING DISHES

PLATE STYLES
Creamware is ideal for regular use, while elegant white with marbled edging suits more formal occasions. If you want a change buy some inexpensive solid-colored plates.

MOST OF US HAVE ONLY ONE whole set of china backed up by a motley collection of unmatching plates, bowls, and dishes for everyday eating. If you entertain a great deal, the ideal situation is to have two whole sets, each with 12 settings. One is for everyday use, and should include serving pieces. This set can be used for informal entertaining. The second could be a grander, more special affair for formal occasions.

BUYING NEW DISHES

Starting afresh with new tableware is both exciting and daunting. The choice available is enormous, so it is important to reflect on what might affect your final decision. First, consider your lifestyle: there is little point in buying expensive china when you usually eat informally around the kitchen table; similarly, if you prefer to entertain in style, chunky plates in bright colors may not be that appropriate. Today, buying dishwasher-proof tableware puts little design restriction on choice, so it is a disinct advantage. Take note of the shapes and sizes of the plates in a given pattern. Soup bowls should always be a good size, and I believe dinner plates are comfortable at about 10in (25cm) in diameter. Larger than this, they are awkward to wash and store;

smaller, and the plate can look overcrowded. I find that flat dessert plates are often much more useful than bowls, and side plates should be large enough to serve salad on. Salad bowls are best in wood and pottery. Three covered serving dishes, a large carving plate, and two sauce boats are important extras.

THE FOOD ON THE PLATE

As the appearance of food varies enormously, there is much to be said for choosing very plain china. For everyday, a stylish all-white or cream plate with some interesting molding, such as fluting or scalloped edges, is hard to beat; most food looks attractive against white. Plates of all one color, particularly yellow, green, and pale blue, also set off food well. Rich, bright colors can look splendid with some dishes, but horrendous with others. Choose them as inexpensive, lighthearted alternatives to more versatile but perhaps less exciting tableware.

IMPROVISE WITH WHAT YOU HAVE

Almost all china can look good on an attractively set out table. To make the most of what you already own, echo the colors in it, in lighter or darker shades, elsewhere on the table. Do not be afraid to mix and match plates of a similar style if you do not have enough of one design: use the napkins, flowers, or candles to provide a link.

Look beyond your usual dishes to find alternative vessels, and introduce unusual elements to reinforce a theme: a large seashell for salt on a nautical table, or a hand-crafted ice bowl from which to serve sorbet or ice cream. Presentation is very important, and it is amazing how you can create a completely new look with what you already have.

FOOD PRESENTATION
When you are deciding on which plates to serve each course, consider how to display the colors and textures of the served food to best advantage.

WHICH GLASS?

GLASSES ARE AVAILABLE for every type of drink from Champagne to cider, from Rully to Friuli, from bitter to stout, from Cloudy Bay to Beyond My Wildest Dreams, and from piña colada to tequila sunrise. You would need an enormous range of glassware to satisfy your thirsty guests in precisely the right glass, so I recommend you choose just a few types to cover the drinks served most often. For the cocktail hour, you may need a set of Champagne flutes; tall tumblers such as a Collins glass for soft drinks, water, long mixed drinks, and beer; low tumblers for whiskey; and sherry glasses. During the meal, large-bowled red wine glasses, good-sized white wine glasses, and water glasses will suffice. Afterward, you may need brandy glasses, port glasses, and liqueur glasses. All others are luxuries. I like clear, colorless glasses best, particularly for serving wine, but there is an ever-widening selection of most attractive colored glasses available for when you would like a change of scene.

WHAT TO SERVE WHEN

For before a meal, I usually make up a pitcher of one drink, such as mimosa, rum punch, or vodka and cranberry juice. This simplifies serving, particularly if you are greeting new arrivals at the same time, and you can always provide a separately prepared drink for anyone who does not like your choice. Always offer a soft alternative such as fruit punch.

On special occasions, it is a great treat to serve more than one wine with the meal; this is not necessary for informal meals. Have a plentiful supply of mineral water, too. Finish off by serving a brandy, port, or liqueur with coffee, perhaps away from the table to help structure the event. When entertaining casually, stemmed multipurpose glasses can be used for most before-meal drinks, red or white wine, and water.

COLLINS LOW TUMBLER MARTINI SHERRY CHAMPAGNE COCKTAIL BEER MULTIPURPOSE STEMMED

APERITIFS △
The Collins, beer, and multi-purpose stemmed glasses are interchangeable, while some cocktail glasses are similar enough to Martini glasses to double for both drinks.

WHITE WINE HOCK INEXPENSIVE RED OR WHITE RED WINE WATER

WITH DINNER △
For most meals, the white wine glass first left, the large-bowled red wine glass, and a water glass are quite adequate. Others are refinements.

△AFTER-DINNER DRINKS
Serve port, and more importantly brandy, in a glass that curves in, to concentrate the aroma. A handled glass suits Irish coffees and hot toddies. Liqueurs are served in small stemmed glasses.

PORT IRISH COFFEE LIQUEUR BRANDY

13

FLOWERS TO IMPRESS A daisy is

ARRANGING FLOWERS
Do this well ahead, leaving you time to perfect the food.

SCHEDULE
Buy flowers about three days in advance, condition them, and store in buckets until you are ready to arrange them.

THE PRESENCE OF FLOWERS lends a grace to any and every occasion. Choose your flowers carefully, then take the time to condition them to make sure they look at their best for your party. A few basic items of equipment are essential. For informal displays, you will need a good pair of florists' scissors, a pair of pruners for cutting woody stems, a small, sharp knife for scraping stems, and buckets in which to condition flowers (use pitchers or vases for smaller flowers). For more complex arrangements, you may need florists' foam, chicken wire, stub wires, wire cutters, florists' gum, and prongs.

FLOWER CHOICE

First decide on the type of arrangement (or arrangements) you want at your party. Where would you like to display it? How much space is available? What vases or other receptacles do you have? What flowers are in season? Do they tie in with, or can they dictate your color scheme? Low displays are most suitable for the table, but larger bold ones can really impress; either have one on the dining table until guests sit down to eat or place on a side table or mantelpiece. Gain inspiration from the gallery on the right, which

INDIVIDUAL TREATMENT

All flowers and foliage should be conditioned as described opposite, but certain plant types need additional special treatment. The hard stems of woody shrubs must be cut at an angle as usual, then the base of each stem split up center, so it takes up water more efficiently. Scrape 2in (5cm) of the bark as usual.

Milky-sapped plants, such as euphorbia and poppy, need to be seared in a flame once cut to stop them from weeping. Cut flowers may have been seared by the florist already.

Some plants, most notably tulips, Corsican hellebore, and privet, are so acidic they adversely affect other flowers, so are best displayed alone.

every bit as beautiful as an orchid

shows the range of displays in the book, for ideas for table, individual place setting, side table, wall, and mantelpiece arrangements.

CONDITIONING

I usually buy flowers three days in advance of the occasion, selecting specimens that are just beyond the bud stage, with healthy fresh leaves. Check stems that have been underwater are not white or pale and are free of slimy bacteria.

When you return home, prepare all plant material by cutting the ends of the stems at a sharp angle and scraping 2in (5cm) around each stem up from the base. Remove any leaves that will be submerged in the final arrangement, and plunge the flowers or foliage into a bucket of water with three or four drops of household bleach added (this inhibits the bacteria that causes plants to rot). Leave in a cool, light (not sunny) place for at least two hours, but preferably overnight or until buds have opened and you do the arrangement, ideally the day before the event. Keep the buckets in a cool place to prolong the plant material's life.

Once arranged, change the water regularly, adding a few drops of bleach each time. Drooping stems are sometimes revived by placing their ends into almost boiling water for five to ten minutes.

FLOWER GALLERY

pages 66–7

pages 30–1

page 64

pages 49–51

pages 72–3

pages 46–7

pages 108–9

pages 126–27

page 142

page 141

pages 110–11

page 157

page 33

page 170

pages 172–73

LIGHTING

THE NATURE AND LEVEL of lighting plays a key role in creating the right atmosphere for your entertainment – it can definitely make or break an occasion. During the day you have less control; though inside, blinds are effective for shading intrusive rays of sun through windows, and on gloomy days candlelight can be most welcome. Outside, for the sake of both guests and the food, the area where you sit and eat should be shaded. Some of my most memorable meals have been enjoyed outside in the soft dappled shade of a vine canopy.

CANDLE EFFECT

In the evening, candles give a soft and flattering light that creates an easy ambience in which people seem to flourish. Candlelight alone may not be sufficient to serve and eat by, so add a little gentle electric illumination to make sure the level of brightness feels just right.

Besides using candlesticks and candelabras, consider including candles in floral displays, or make lanterns. Outside, candles need to be protected from a breeze. Although glass candle protectors are readily available, you can improvise your own by placing candles in drinking glasses. Remember that scented candles, such as rosemary, citronella, and lemon, are excellent at keeping insects away.

TABLE DISPLAYS

pages 72–3   *pages 124–25*   *pages 140–41*

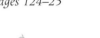

pages 68–9   *page 69*   *page 107*

CANDLE SAFETY

Never leave candles burning unattended. Inside, in particular, light candles only when someone can keep an eye on them. Position them carefully out of the way of individuals serving food, where they will not impede the view across the table, or scorch flower arrangements or walls.

Candles used in displays with fresh flowers are moderately safe because the plant material is unlikely to catch fire, and the container has water in it. Make sure that the candles are always taller than or well away from flowers and leaves.

TABLE LINEN

THE MOST INVITING dinner tables I have seen often owe much of their appeal to the table linen: the cloth and the napkins. Consider the color of the cloth carefully as it dominates the look of the table; I believe in keeping it plain. If you are buying new table linen, neutral colors are the most useful; white, cream, and pale gray are all favorites of mine, but of the darker colors, holly green and rich dark red can look magnificent, especially in winter. Wooden table surfaces are soft and mellow, but it is most important to use place mats to prevent scratches and heat damage to the table. Choose them to co-ordinate with the table decorations and napkins.

THE DETAILS

Much old-fashioned formality has now disappeared, but I am always disappointed if I do not have a crisply laundered plain or damask linen napkin in a restaurant. Cloth napkins engender a great sense of luxury at home, too, and although they may involve more work afterward, their contribution to the overall effect makes them well worth the effort for the majority of occasions. For large parties, paper napkins are more practical, though. I prefer a simple rolled or folded napkin, maybe with a decorative ring or tie.

NAPKIN IDEAS

pages 28–31   pages 156–57   pages 64–5

pages 32–3   pages 46–7   pages 48–9

pages 172–73   pages 142–43   pages 140–41

NAPKIN RINGS

Use braided raffia or ribbon, wire-edged for best effect, to make your own napkin rings. It is very simple, and is a most effective way of linking the assorted decorative elements of your table together.

THE PLACE SETTING Fortunately,

A NAGGING BUT UNNECESSARY CONCERN often surrounds the order in which cutlery should be placed when setting a dining table. The simple convention (below) is that knives, forks, and spoons are placed in course order, from the outside inward, on either side of a central plate. A bread knife is placed on the extreme right. Water and wine glasses stand on the right above the knives, and the side plate with its napkin sits on the left beyond the cutlery. An alternative, particularly if the napkin is decoratively folded or tied (page 17), is to place it on the central plate, with the bread knife on the side plate. If this layout takes up too much space around your table, consider one of the more informal options (right).

FORMAL SETTING
This setting is for four courses: soup, then a savory first course, followed by the main course, and a dessert. Two wines will be served. A charger plate adds to the formality of the setting.

SIDE PLATE
Placed to the left of the main plate, this often has the napkin on it, and is used for bread or salad.

CHARGER PLATE
A optional large decorative plate remains in place throughout the meal.

eating peas off a knife is not easy

WINE GLASSES
The glass used first, usually for white wine, is set closest to the plate.

WATER GLASS
Place this above the knives.

CUTLERY
Arrange in the order of the courses, from the outside in, with extras such as the bread knife on the outside.

ALTERNATE LAYOUT

Table settings can easily be adapted from the conventional one (left) for less formal occasions and to limit the amount of lateral space occupied by each place, perhaps when entertaining more than six people around the average-sized dining table. Two possible alternatives are shown below.

INFORMAL SETTING
Here, the dessert spoon and fork are set above the plate, spoon above fork, with the handles pointing in the direction in which they will be picked up. Place the napkin on the central plate or side plate.

MINIMALIST
Unless the first course and the main course are too divergent in flavor, use the same knife and fork for both. A cutlery rest helps keep the table clean. Use an informal wine glass for wine or water.

SETTING A DINING TABLE

WHEN SETTING A TABLE, your main concern should be the comfort of your guests and the ease with which they can converse with one another. Ideally, I like each individual to be able to talk to everyone present. With more than eight people this can become difficult, unless you have an oval table. Since my dining table is rectangular, the ideal number of guests seems to be six; it gives unity to the group and appears to prevent anyone from feeling isolated. With a larger number seated at a rectangular table, the group often polarizes into two; on such occasions, I ask some guests to swap places between courses.

Some hosts resent missing out on conversation while cooking during the meal, and so prefer to entertain in the kitchen. This also means hot food stays that way between oven and table, but it is an arrangement that may not suit less confident cooks. Bear in mind that the accumulation of debris as the occasion progresses can be unsightly!

SPACE FOR COMFORT

The dining table must never feel crowded. Where space is limited, serve away from the table rather than trying to fit serving bowls in the center. Condiments, bread, and salad should be easily accessible; for more than six people have two salt-and-pepper sets on the table.

An arrangement of flowers, however simple, always makes the table feel well dressed and, certainly for evening meals, the glow of candles adds to the atmosphere. Be sure they do not occupy too much space or obstruct guests' vision lines. I often have a large arrangement on the table until guests sit down, when I move it to a side table for the meal. Small vases at each place are attractive and less intrusive.

▽ THE WELL-DRESSED TABLE
The dining table should never feel intimidating, even for the most elegant of dinners. In every aspect of its decoration, make the comfort of your guests the absolute top priority.

SALT AND PEPPER
Allow one set for every six people; small bowls of coarse salt and coarse pepper are a good alternative.

DINING ERGONOMICS

To enable guests to cut their food and use a fork with ease, allow about 26in (65cm) between the center of each place setting. Leave enough room in the middle of the table for essential condiments. Aim to achieve a balance between enabling your guests to help themselves to items, so you are not continually attending to their needs, and keeping the table uncluttered. If you have flowers and candles on the table, make sure people can see one another clearly over them.

SALAD BOWL
Space now occupied by the salad bowl held an impressive floral display before guests were seated.

FLOWERS
Small, well-balanced vases or bowls hold individual flower arrangements.

WATER PITCHER
A pitcher of bottled or tap water on the table allows guests to help themselves.

SETTING A BUFFET TABLE

AS BUFFETS ARE GENERALLY used for large crowds, easy access is the main requirement of a buffet table. Where possible, have two serving stations (one food, one drink), and make food that is simple to eat and serve.

For a self-service buffet, a table that guests can walk around is ideal, but in many homes space restrictions mean the table will be against a wall, and the line will feed along one side of it, as shown below. Lay items out in the order they are to be collected: the plates, cutlery, and napkins first, followed by the main dishes; any dressings, condiments, bread, and salad

SELF-SERVICE
This buffet of two pasta dishes with salad is set out along the front of a table against a wall so guests can help themselves.

ESSENTIAL TOOLS
Arrange cutlery so that it is easy to pick up.

NAPKINS
Provide sufficient paper napkins for each guest to use more than one.

PASTA BOWLS
Serving dishes for hot food should not be too large; replenish them frequently.

SALAD
For a buffet, choose small salad leaves that are easy to eat.

SALT AND PEPPER
Guests can take pinches of coarse pepper and sea salt: spoons easily tip over small bowls.

should be close by. To save having to set dessert plates and cutlery out during the meal, place them farther down the table, away from the main courses. Place any low flower and candle decorations in inaccessible spaces at the back, or between the items needed for one course and the next. Red wine, or white wine in a cooler, can be judiciously placed for refills, away from the main flow for food.

BREAD AND BUTTER
Cut both the bread and the butter into pieces of manageable size.

FLOWERS
Position a low bowl of flowers where it will not obstruct serving.

DESSERT ITEMS
Bowls, spoons, and cookies await the arrival of ice cream.

CATERING TO A CROWD

The tables below are set for large numbers. An all-around setting allows more guests to help themselves to food at a time than does the table against a wall (left). For more than 18, it is worth stationing someone behind the table to serve the main dishes.

ALL-AROUND ACCESS
As for all buffet settings, set the plates, cutlery, and napkins first. Place main dishes next, with extras such as Parmesan cheese and condiments close at hand. Salad, bread, butter, extra salt and pepper, and drinks with glasses (laid on the table as there is room) follow to complete the circuit.

SERVER BEHIND THE TABLE
The main dishes (at the back of the table) are served by a host or waiter, but guests help themselves to cutlery, napkins, salad, bread, butter, and condiments (all situated at the front of the table). There is space for wine, but not glasses. Ensure that hot food replenishments can arrive without disruption.

COUNTDOWN TO THE EVENT

THE KEY TO KEEPING CALM is having everything well ordered. You will feel much more at ease and, consequently, so will your guests. Making lists may sound dull but, when organizing an event, I cannot do without them.

DECISIONS, LISTS, AND SCHEDULES

Once you have chosen a menu and settled on a theme, make a shopping list of all the ingredients needed, including drinks to be ordered, remembering nonalcoholic drinks, and tea and coffee. Decide on flowers or other special items like candles that you may require and add these to your shopping list. Next, plan a detailed cooking schedule, always including early preparation tasks such as marinating.

Now is the time to consider the format of the actual occasion itself. Plan exactly where each stage of the event should take place, from premeal drinks to coffee afterward. When this is decided, make a second schedule of noncooking tasks such as arranging flowers, preparing any special items, setting the table, tidying up, and drawing up a seating plan. Include on this list reminders of tasks to be done during the event, too, such as adjusting the central heating, preheating the oven, or removing sorbet from the freezer to soften. Closer to the event, it may help to combine your cooking and noncooking schedules.

FIRST DRINKS
Set out drinks and glasses in readiness for pouring as soon as your guests arrive.

SHOPPING
Plan to shop more than once; this allows you to purchase items that were unavailable or that you may have forgotten to buy first time around.

"Perfection is the child

THE TIME APPROACHES

While cooking, I frequently find a second timer is a useful reminder of noncooking tasks that still need to be completed. Try, if you can, to leave plenty of time for any glitches, as well as a restorative tea or coffee break. Strike out the jobs on your lists as you complete them – this is both satisfying and reassuring.

Make sure that each space you will be using is neat and welcoming, and set up what you need in each room before everyone arrives. Set a drink tray in readiness, and place cups and saucers where you plan to serve coffee. Decide on a division of tasks if more than one of you is hosting the event.

LAST-MINUTE PANIC

Remember to allow enough time to get yourself ready. There is bound to be some last-minute cooking, however much you prepare in advance, but a few minutes of relaxation with a drink before the doorbell rings is a lifesaver.

of time." JOSEPH HALL 1574–1656

SCHEDULE

▷ SEVERAL WEEKS BEFORE
　Decide to have a party
　Consider who to invite
　Issue invitations
　Choose a menu
　Hire any help or rent necessary equipment

▷ THE WEEK BEFORE
　Prepare food, drink, and flowers shopping list
　Write out party schedule
　Cook food that can be frozen
　Decide rooms in which you will entertain

▷ THREE DAYS BEFORE
　Buy and condition flowers
　Make relevant table decorations
　Buy drinks

▷ THE PREVIOUS DAY
　Shop for food
　Arrange flowers
　Tidy up and iron table linen
　Make sure you have a good supply of ice
　Prepare food that can be kept overnight

▷ THE DAY OF THE PARTY
　Prepare as much food in advance as possible
　Do all cooking that can be reheated
　　at the last minute
　Prepare rooms where you will be entertaining
　Set out drink tray
　Bring wines to correct temperatures

▷ A FEW HOURS BEFORE
　Set table
　Decide on seating plan
　Start any early cooking

▷ THE LAST HOUR
　Have as much cooking as possible underway
　Straighten up kitchen; wash dishes
　Get yourself ready
　Open red wines to breathe
　Take a short break – you deserve it!

▷ AT THE PARTY
　For lunch or dinner parties, allow 1¼ hours
　from the first guest arriving to starting the meal

BREAKFAST & BRUNCH

THE FIRST MEAL OF THE DAY IS A PARTICULAR AND SPECIAL ONE, AWAKENING APPETITES ANEW. SERVED AS A HEARTY FAMILY FEAST, A SPREAD FOR A CASUAL GATHERING OF FRIENDS, OR AN INTIMATE REPAST FOR TWO, IT SHOULD ALWAYS BE HOMEY, RELAXED, AND INFORMAL. THE DISHES ARE ONES OF WHICH WE NEVER TIRE: I SO RELISH THE TASTE-PACKED MIX OF THESE SIMPLE FOODS THAT I AM OFTEN TEMPTED TO PREPARE THEM FOR LUNCH AND DINNER, TOO!

A rustic outdoor setting (right) provides the perfect context for the delicious flavors of the Late Summer Brunch menu (page 34).

RUSTIC

A beautiful morning, and the air is buzzing

CREATE A RUSTIC Provençal atmosphere, perfect for a late breakfast or even later brunch, with golden tableware set on a sky-blue plank table.

LINING A BASKET
Use a good-sized napkin or tea cloth to line a basket for your breakfast rolls, toast, or chunks of bread. This flowerlike liner will keep bread deliciously warm.

SKY-BLUE TABLE
This plank table is painted with a blue wash. If you have an old wooden table, give it one coat to complement your tableware.

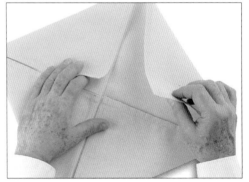

1 Spread a large square napkin, right side facing down, on a table or other flat surface. Fold each of the four corners to meet exactly in the center.

2 Preserving the folds you have made, carefully turn the napkin over and fold each corner to meet exactly in the center once again.

3 Place in the basket, holding down the ends in the center. Bring each loose corner up from underneath, making a flowery nest for your bread rolls.

Find the loose corners and bring them over

with promise

SLAB OF BUTTER
A chunk of farm-fresh butter on a pottery dish needs no fussy arranging; its uneven form makes it tempting.

BREAD BASKET
Wicker has an easy informality that is suited to most daytime eating; add a flower-folded napkin to keep the bread warm.

RAFFIA TIES
Choose plain napkins that complement the color of your dishes. Secure each one with a braided raffia tie (page 31).

EVOKE SUNSHINE IN THE DETAILS

MORNING FLOWERS

Simple flower arrangements are most appropriate for a relaxed breakfast or brunch. Every season offers a range of plant material, particularly if you select flowers, leaves, and berries for their textures as well as their colors. The color scheme of these two summer displays is drawn from the warm sunny shades of the dishes on page 28. If at all possible, choose flowers that complement your own tableware.

Butterfly weed

CALENDULA BASKET
Some flower species, such as these calendulas, offer a range of shades in the same color band. A yellow basket, lined to make it waterproof, shows them off most attractively.

COLOR HARMONY
Rich orange provides an important foil to the bright yellow, lime green, and red of the other plants.

The secret is natural, homespun simplicity

NAPKIN FANS

Neutral-colored napkin ties made from braided raffia will suit any rustic daytime feast. I have teamed them here with sunny yellow linen napkins, but all weights of cotton will work well.

1 Fold one third of a square linen napkin in and smooth down. Make small, even accordion folds at right angles to the initial fold to form a fan; you can iron these in.

2 Divide about 30 strands of raffia, 14in (35cm) in length, into three, and braid. Secure each end with a single strand, and knot the tie around the bulky end of the napkin fan.

Dill

Calendula

St. John's wort

Miniature sunflower

WEATHERED CONTAINER
This old watering can makes an exciting rustic container. I have lined it with a plastic bucket to make sure it stays watertight.

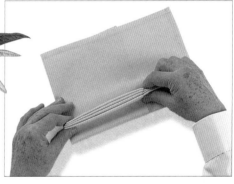

INDULGENT

Breakfast together, companions forever

FOR A LUXURIANT and intimate breakfast in bed, set trays in advance, have the brioche ready to warm, champagne chilled, and the coffeepot waiting.

LOVER'S ROSE HEART

Ensure a romantic start to the day by making a simple, sweet-scented heart to grace the breakfast tray. Moss frames the flowers, and galax leaves adorn the sides.

CAFETIERE
Be sure to make enough richly aromatic coffee for two cups each.

1 Wrap the base and sides of a piece of soaked florists' foam in plastic. Trim the plastic to fit, and secure with adhesive tape.

2 Cut one side of each galax leaf straight, to align with the base of the foam. Apply glue along the straight edge.

3 Glue each leaf to the side of the heart. Pin the unglued top part to the foam, but do not pierce the base or it will leak.

4 Overlap the leaves all the way around, to completely cover the sides. Trim the rose stems to 1in (2.5cm) each, and stick in the center of the foam shape. Tuck a ruff of Spanish moss between the leaves and roses to finish the heart.

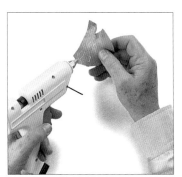

Secure moss and stray leaves with pins

ROSE IN A NAPKIN
*Fold a large linen napkin
into a triangle, then wrap
it around a single rose.*

LINEN TRAY CLOTH
*As a tray cloth, use a linen
napkin that matches the
one holding the rose.*

LEMON CURD
*Spoon an individual
portion of homemade
lemon curd into a small
bowl for the tray.*

MENUS

Good food in the morning makes the rest

WHOLESOME START

Impress a small crowd, or just a few close friends, with this colorful cosmopolitan menu. *Serves 6*

MANGO & PAPAYA
A bright fan of exotic fruits with a squeeze of lime.

PROVENÇAL PIPÉRADE
An easy-to-make French omelet, encapsulating flavors of the Mediterranean.

CRANBERRY MUFFINS
Delicious muffins with a cranberry kick.

DRINKS
A large pitcher of cranberry juice to start, and an invigorating rosehip or hibiscus tisane to accompany the meal.

PLANNING NOTES
Make the muffins and lightly cook the pipérade vegetables the day before. Early in the day, slice the mango and papaya, squeezing the lime juice over them to prevent discoloration. Pipérade is best eaten fresh, so assemble it during the meal, using two pans if you are making more than six portions. *See pages 36–7 for recipes.*

LATE SUMMER BRUNCH

The tantalizing flavors and colors of this alfresco country feast are just reward for the time spent preparing it. *Serves 12*

PERNOD PEARS IN GRAPEFRUIT JUICE
The piquant juice is perfect with pears.

PROSCIUTTO, SHRIMP & APPLES
Best enjoyed freshly made; a delicious combination.

GOLDEN CORN & GREEN PEA PANCAKES
Tasty by themselves, these pancakes are a good base for the prosciutto, shrimp, and apples.

DRINKS
One part Campari to six parts ruby orange juice makes a refreshing start. Offer hot Arabica coffee throughout the meal.

PLANNING NOTES
Prepare the Pernod pears a day ahead to allow the flavors to develop. Pancakes freeze well, so you can make them several days in advance; defrost the night before, and reheat in a hot oven before serving. Cook the prosciutto, shrimp, and apples just before serving, after making or reheating the pancakes. *See pages 38–9 for recipes.*

of the day a pleasure

LOVERS' BREAKFAST

Indulge in the exciting colors, spicy tastes, and interesting textures of this exotic breakfast menu.
Serves 2

COEUR À LA CRÈME & PASSION FRUIT
Make a romantic start to the day with heart-shaped molds of farmer cheese and yogurt.

SPICY KEDGEREE
A successful mix of smoked fish and spicy rice.

RICH LEMON CURD
Creamy lemon curd tastes wonderful on a light-textured bread such as brioche.

DRINKS
Mix two-thirds Champagne and one-third freshly squeezed orange juice to celebrate the new day. End with strong Arabica coffee.

PLANNING NOTES
Lemon curd can be made well in advance and lasts for up to three months in the refrigerator. The coeur à la crème must be made the day before to allow it to drip overnight. Prepare the kedgeree the day before; simply heat it through in a moderate oven for 12 minutes just before serving, while you are squeezing the oranges to go with the champagne.
See pages 40–1 for recipes.

WINTER BREAKFAST

The traditional hearty breakfast is one of those great meals. Serve this refined version at weekends as a leisurely treat for some special guests.
Serves 6

BUBBLE & SQUEAK
Coarsely crushed potatoes and cabbage, with bacon, baked crisp and golden.

HERBED TOMATOES
Tomato halves, baked with sprigs of wild herbs.

CREAMY SCRAMBLED EGGS
Delicious comfort food, best served immediately after cooking.

TOAST WITH ORANGE & LIME MARMALADE
Lightly toasted whole-grain bread complements this elegant preserve.

DRINKS
A large cafetiere of Kenya coffee, refreshed frequently.

PLANNING NOTES
Prepare the bubble and squeak ingredients the day before, but do not bake. On the day, bake the bubble and squeak, and chop the herbs for the tomatoes. Bake the tomatoes and make the scrambled eggs while the bubble and squeak is cooking, immediately before eating. *See pages 42–3 for recipes.*

WHOLESOME START FOR 6

MANGO & PAPAYA

🍲 15 MINUTES

INGREDIENTS
3 LARGE RIPE MANGOES
2 LARGE RIPE PAPAYA
2 LIMES, JUICE ONLY
SUPERFINE SUGAR TO TASTE (OPTIONAL)
MINT SPRIGS TO GARNISH

1 Peel the mangoes with a potato peeler and cut each one into 6 slices, slicing lengthwise, parallel to the flat side of the pit.

2 Peel the papaya, cut in half lengthwise, then scoop out and discard the seeds. Cut each piece of fruit into 9 slices across the width of each half.

3 Arrange 3 slices of mango and 3 slices of papaya on each plate in a fan shape and drizzle lime juice over each serving. For a sweeter salad, sprinkle a little superfine sugar over the top. Garnish with a sprig of mint.

COOK'S TIP
Pineapple, kiwi fruit, or banana can be used in addition to, or instead of, the mango and papaya. This delicious dish also makes a simple and refreshing dessert.

PROVENÇAL
PIPÉRADE

PROVENÇAL PIPÉRADE

☑ 10 MINUTES 🍲 20 MINUTES

INGREDIENTS

3 TBSP OLIVE OIL
½ LB (250G) SMOKED HAM, CUT INTO
1 IN (2.5CM) STRIPS
4 SHALLOTS, THINLY SLICED
1 RED PEPPER, THINLY SLICED
1 GARLIC CLOVE, CRUSHED
2 TSP FRESH THYME (PREFERABLY LEMON
THYME), FINELY CHOPPED
3 PLUM TOMATOES, PEELED, & CHOPPED
3 NEW POTATOES, SCRUBBED,
COOKED, & DICED
SALT & PEPPER TO TASTE
2 TBSP BUTTER
12 EGGS, LIGHTLY BEATEN

1 Heat 1 tablespoon of the oil in a skillet. Add the ham and cook for about 2 minutes on each side, until just brown. Transfer to a warmed dish to keep hot in the oven.

2 Add the shallots, red pepper, garlic, and thyme to the pan, and cook over a moderate heat for about 10 minutes, until just softened.

3 Add the tomatoes and potatoes and continue to cook for about 15 minutes, until all the liquid has been absorbed. Adjust seasoning.

4 Heat the remaining oil and the butter in a large skillet. Pour in the eggs and stir until softly scrambled. Remove the pan from the heat and spoon the vegetable mixture over the eggs. Finally, top with the warm ham and sprinkle with coarse ground black pepper. Serve immediately with lightly buttered toast.

COOK'S TIP
The vegetable mixture can be prepared a day in advance and just warmed gently in a saucepan. The ham and eggs, however, should be cooked immediately before serving.

CRANBERRY MUFFINS

☑ 20 MINUTES 🍲 20 MINUTES

INGREDIENTS

1 CUP (75G) ROLLED OATS
1 CUP (200ML) MILK, WARMED
8 TBSP (120G) ALL-PURPOSE FLOUR
½ TSP BAKING SODA
1½ TSP BAKING POWDER
PINCH OF SALT
1 LARGE EGG, LIGHTLY BEATEN
6 TBSP (90G) LIGHT BROWN SUGAR
2 TBSP BUTTER, MELTED
⅓ CUP (90G) CRANBERRIES OR ½ CUP (60G)
BLUEBERRIES, COARSELY CHOPPED

1 Preheat oven to 400°F/200°C. Place the oats in a large mixing bowl and pour over the milk. Stir well and set aside for 10–15 minutes to cool.

2 Meanwhile, in another mixing bowl, sift together the flour, baking soda, baking powder, and salt. Add the egg and sugar to the oatmeal mixture and beat well. Stir in the sifted ingredients, alternating with the butter and cranberries.

3 Divide the mixture among 12 x 3in (7.5cm) muffin tins or strong paper muffin cups. Bake for 18–20 minutes, until golden. Leave the muffins in their tins for about 5 minutes, then turn them out onto a wire rack. Serve warm with unsalted butter.

COOK'S TIP
For sweeter muffins, use the fresh blueberries instead of cranberries.

CRANBERRY
MUFFINS

LATE SUMMER BRUNCH FOR 12

PERNOD PEARS IN GRAPEFRUIT JUICE

20 MINUTES   30 MINUTES

INGREDIENTS
12 PEARS, NOT QUITE RIPE
4½ CUPS (1 LITER) PINK GRAPEFRUIT JUICE
⅓ CUP (90G) SUPERFINE SUGAR
12 STAR ANISE
¾ CUP (175ML) ANISE LIQUEUR
(PREFERABLY PERNOD)

1 Halve, peel, and core the pears. Place in a large saucepan, pour over the grapefruit juice, and add the sugar and star anise.

2 Bring to boil, cover, and simmer for about 15–20 minutes, until the pears are just tender.

3 Transfer the pears to a serving dish. Boil down the juice left in the pan until it has reduced by about half.

4 Strain the juice into a large measuring cup and let cool. Add the Pernod. Pour the liquid over the pears and refrigerate until needed.

COOK'S TIP
These pears can be prepared the day before they are required. For a nonalcoholic alternative to Pernod try ginger ale, or ginger cordial, omitting the sugar from the recipe.

PROSCIUTTO, SHRIMP & APPLES

10 MINUTES   20 MINUTES

INGREDIENTS
6 CRISP RED EATING APPLES (PREFERABLY
JONAGOLD)
½ LEMON, JUICE ONLY
2½ TBSP SUGAR
1 LB (500G) LARGE SHRIMP
7 TBSP (105ML) VEGETABLE OIL
10 SPRIGS EACH FRESH
THYME & MARJORAM
SALT & PEPPER TO TASTE
1 LB (500G) PROSCIUTTO, VERY THINLY SLICED
½ LB (250G) MIXED MUSHROOMS, SLICED

1 Preheat oven to the lowest setting. Cut each apple into 12 slices and remove the core. Place the slices in a bowl and sprinkle with the lemon juice and sugar. Prepare the shrimp (see Step 1, page 94).

2 Heat 3 tablespoons of the oil in a large skillet and cook the apples with the herbs for about 5 minutes, until golden. Season lightly. Transfer to a warmed dish to keep hot in the oven.

3 Cook the prosciutto slices in the pan for about 5 minutes, until crisp, turning frequently. Place on a baking sheet and keep warm in the oven.

4 Heat the remaining olive oil in the same skillet, and sauté the mushrooms for about 5 minutes. Remove with a slotted spoon and place with the prosciutto slices in the oven.

5 In the same oil, sauté the shrimp for about 2 minutes, until they turn pink. Transfer everything to a large serving dish and and serve with Golden Corn & Green Pea Pancakes (see opposite).

COOK'S TIP
The cooking times for the apples and mushrooms will vary according to the varieties used. They both need to be *al dente* and not overcooked.

GOLDEN CORN & GREEN PEA PANCAKES

🥄 10 MINUTES 🍳 35 MINUTES 🍽 30 MINUTES CHILLING

INGREDIENTS

1¼ CUPS (175G) ALL-PURPOSE FLOUR, SIFTED
1¼ CUPS (175G) CORNMEAL, SIFTED
½ LB PLUS 2 TBSP (275G) BUTTER
3¾ CUPS (900ML) MILK
6 EGGS, LIGHTLY BEATEN
12OZ (350G) FROZEN CORN KERNELS, THAWED
8OZ (250G) FROZEN PETIT POIS, THAWED
3 TBSP EACH OF FRESH PARSLEY &
CHIVES, COARSELY CHOPPED
1½ TBSP FINELY CHOPPED FRESH THYME
SALT & PEPPER TO TASTE
SALAD GREENS & CRÈME FRAÎCHE OR
SOUR CREAM TO SERVE

COOK'S TIP

These pancakes can be cooked a day in advance. To warm again for serving, arrange on 2 or 3 large baking sheets, wrap the sheets loosely with foil, and reheat in a moderate oven for about 15 minutes.

1 In a large bowl, mix the flour and cornmeal. Heat 4 tablespoons of the butter to melting point.

2 Gradually whisk the milk, eggs, and melted butter into the flour mixture. Stir in the corn, peas, herbs, and seasoning. Cover and refrigerate for at least 30 minutes. Stir.

3 Place 2 teaspoons of the remaining butter into a 25cm (10in) skillet and heat until the butter just browns.

4 Put 2 tablespoons of batter into the pan. Cook for approximately 1 minute on each side, until golden. Transfer to a wire rack in the oven to keep warm, and repeat with the remaining batter.

5 Place the pancakes on a bed of salad greens and serve with Prosciutto, Shrimp & Apples (see opposite) and a dollop of crème fraîche, or with bacon and maple syrup.

PROSCIUTTO, SHRIMP & APPLES

GOLDEN CORN & GREEN PEA PANCAKES

LOVERS' BREAKFAST FOR 2

COEUR À LA CRÈME & PASSION FRUIT

15 MINUTES   12 HOURS COOLING

INGREDIENTS
6 TBSP (120ML) COTTAGE CHEESE
4 TBSP LOW-FAT CREAM CHEESE
6 TBSP (120ML) LOW-FAT PLAIN YOGURT
1 TBSP SUPERFINE SUGAR
1 TSP VANILLA EXTRACT
1 LARGE EGG, WHITE ONLY
2 PASSION FRUITS
1 TBSP CONFECTIONERS' SUGAR, SIFTED
SOFT FRUITS TO DECORATE

COOK'S TIP
A raspberry or strawberry coulis makes a delicious alternative to passion fruit.

1 Beat together the cottage cheese, cream cheese, yogurt, superfine sugar, and vanilla until well mixed.

2 Beat the egg white until it forms stiff peaks. Fold gradually into the cheese mixture.

3 Line *coeur à la crème* molds (heart-shaped ceramic molds with holes in the base) with muslin or cheesecloth and spoon in the mixture. If molds are unavailable, use small yogurt or cream containers with holes pierced in the bottom. Let drain on a tray in the refrigerator for at least 12 hours.

4 To make the coulis, halve the passion fruits and scoop out the flesh. Rub the flesh through a sieve to remove the seeds. Add the confectioners' sugar to the purée and mix well.

5 Turn out of the molds onto a serving plate. Drizzle the sauce around the crème (about 1 tablespoon per person) and serve with soft fruits.

COEUR À LA CRÈME &
PASSION FRUIT

SPICY
KEDGEREE

SPICY KEDGEREE

☑ 10 MINUTES ⌣ 20–30 MINUTES

INGREDIENTS

1 CUP (200G) BASMATI RICE
1 TBSP OLIVE OIL
2 TBSP BUTTER
1 TBSP MILD CURRY POWDER
6 CARDAMOMS, SEEDS CRUSHED
2 TSP GROUND CUMIN
2 SHALLOTS, FINELY CHOPPED
½ LB (200G) FISH (COD, WHITING, OR HAKE),
BONED, SKINNED, & FLAKED
LARGE PINCH OF GROUND SAFFRON
2 CUPS (500ML) FISH STOCK (SEE PAGE 185)
2 EGGS, HARD BOILED, PEELED, & CHOPPED
2 TBSP CRÈME FRAÎCHE OR LIGHT SOUR CREAM
LUMPFISH ROE & SPRIGS FRESH PARSLEY
TO GARNISH

1 Rinse the rice in a sieve under cold running water until the water runs completely clear.

2 Heat the olive oil and butter in a saucepan. Add the curry powder, cardamom, cumin, and shallots. Cook gently, stirring, for 5 minutes, until the shallots are softened.

3 Add the rice, fish, and saffron and stir until the rice is completely coated in the oil, then add the stock. Bring to a boil, stir, and then turn the heat to very low. Cover tightly and cook undisturbed for 8 minutes.

4 Remove the rice from the heat, stir once, and fluff up with a fork. The rice should be separated into grains and *al dente*.

5 Add the eggs to the rice and fish mixture, then add the crème fraîche. Stir well. Serve with a garnish of lumpfish roe and several sprigs of fresh parsley.

COOK'S TIP

The kedgeree can be made the day before and refrigerated. Reheat it in a moderate oven for 15 minutes before serving.

RICH LEMON CURD

☑ 10 MINUTES ⌣ 30–40 MINUTES

INGREDIENTS

8 EGGS, YOLKS ONLY
1 CUP (250G) SUPERFINE SUGAR
5 LEMONS, JUICE & GRATED ZEST
1¼ CUPS (150G) UNSALTED BUTTER,
CHILLED & IN PIECES
3 x (8OZ) 250G JARS

1 Place the egg yolks and sugar in a double boiler, or a heatproof bowl over a saucepan of simmering water. Gently beat for about 10 minutes, until the mixture begins to thicken.

2 Beat in the lemon juice and zest, then gradually add the butter, a piece at a time. Continue to beat for 20–30 minutes, until thickened. Do not allow the mixture to boil or it will separate.

3 Spoon the mixture into sterilized jars. Cover the tops of the jars with disks of waxed paper, and tightly seal them. Let cool, then refrigerate the jars until needed. Serve with slightly warmed brioche.

COOK'S TIP

Lemon curd will keep for up to 3 months in the refrigerator.

WINTER BREAKFAST FOR 6

BUBBLE & SQUEAK

20 MINUTES   45 MINUTES

INGREDIENTS

1½ LB (750G) POTATOES, PEELED
1 TBSP OLIVE OIL, PLUS EXTRA FOR DRIZZLING
3OZ (90G) SLICED SMOKED PANCETTA OR BACON
2 LEEKS, THINLY SLICED
12OZ (375G) SAVOY CABBAGE, SHREDDED
SALT & PEPPER TO TASTE
7 TBSP (100G) BUTTER, IN PIECES

COOK'S TIP

This may be prepared, but not baked, a day ahead. Cover the baking dish with plastic wrap and refrigerate overnight. Bake for an extra 5–10 minutes.

1 Preheat oven to 450°F/220°C. Place the potatoes in a saucepan of cold water, bring to boil, cover, and simmer for 12 minutes, until cooked.

2 Meanwhile, heat the olive oil in a large skillet and cook the pancetta for 10 minutes, until crisp. Drain on paper towels.

3 Cook the leeks and cabbage in a large pan of salted boiling water for 4 minutes, until *al dente*. Refresh under cold water and drain.

4 When the potatoes are cooked, drain and then mash well. Stir in the pancetta, leeks, and cabbage and adjust seasoning.

5 Spoon the mixture into a large greased baking dish, dot with butter, and drizzle with olive oil. Bake in the oven for 20–25 minutes, until brown on top.

HERBED
TOMATOES

BUBBLE &
SQUEAK

CREAMY
SCRAMBLED EGGS

HERBED TOMATOES

5 MINUTES 20 MINUTES

INGREDIENTS
3 LARGE TOMATOES (PREFERABLY BEEFSTEAK)
1 TBSP HONEY
1 TBSP EACH FRESH THYME & PARSLEY,
FINELY CHOPPED
2 TBSP BUTTER
SALT & PEPPER TO TASTE

1 Preheat oven to 450°F/220°C. Cut each tomato in half and remove the core from the center. Place in an ovenproof dish, cut side up.

2 Combine the remaining ingredients in a mixing bowl. Spread the herb mixture over the tomato halves and bake in the oven for 15–20 minutes, until crisp on top.

COOK'S TIP
The tomatoes can be cooked in the oven with the Bubble & Squeak (see opposite).

CREAMY SCRAMBLED EGGS

5 MINUTES 4 MINUTES

INGREDIENTS
12 EGGS
SALT & PEPPER TO TASTE
4 TBSP BUTTER
6 TBSP (90ML) HEAVY CREAM

1 Lightly beat the eggs and seasoning until mixed but not foamy.

2 Melt the butter in a skillet or saucepan over low heat. Add the eggs and stir constantly until they start to thicken and are the consistency of soft whipped cream.

3 Remove from the heat and add the cream. Stir well. Serve immediately.

COOK'S TIP
It is always best to cook with eggs that are at room temperature.

ORANGE & LIME MARMALADE

1 HOUR 15 MINUTES 6 HOURS 30 MINUTES 6 HOURS COOLING

INGREDIENTS
8 ORANGES (PREFERABLY SEVILLE)
6 LIMES
3 LEMONS
10 CUPS (2.5KG) SUGAR

COOK'S TIPS
If you have a candy thermometer, the temperature needed for setting is 219°F/104°C. Let it stand for 15 minutes and stir before pouring to prevent the fruit from rising to top. The recipe makes about 8lb (4kg) of marmalade.

1 Place the whole oranges, limes, and lemons in a large saucepan or preserving pan and cover with water. Bring to a boil, cover, and simmer over very low heat for 6 hours. Let cool, covered, for 6 hours longer.

2 Cut the fruits in half, remove and discard the seeds, and coarsely chop. Reserve 5 cups (1.25 liters) of the liquid in the pan.

3 Add the chopped fruits and sugar to the pan and place over medium heat, stirring constantly, until the sugar dissolves. Bring to a boil.

4 After 15 minutes, test the mixture to see if the marmalade is ready: place a teaspoon of the mixture on a chilled plate and put it in the freezer for 1 minute – if the liquid jells on the plate, it is ready. If not, repeat the test every 2 minutes until it has set (it may take up to 30 minutes). Remove the marmalade from the heat.

5 Pour the marmalade into sterilized jars. Cover the tops of the jars with disks of waxed paper and tightly seal them. Store in the refrigerator.

LUNCH

RELAXING MEALS IN THE MIDDLE OF THE DAY ARE ALL TOO OFTEN NEGLECTED, THANKS TO THE HECTIC PACE OF MODERN LIVING. YET THEY CAN BE ONE OF LIFE'S GREAT PLEASURES, SINCE OUR APPETITES ARE AT THEIR SHARPEST AT NOON. THE WEEKEND BECOMES IDEAL FOR A SIMPLE BUT DELICIOUS MEAL WITH FAMILY AND FRIENDS. ONCE FOOD AND WINE HAVE BEEN SAVORED, PLENTY OF TIME IS LEFT FOR INDULGING IN LEISURELY CONVERSATION, A WALK, OR EVEN A SIESTA.

For a tempting, exotic lunch party, team the interesting textures and spicy tastes of the Oriental Flavors menu (page 52), with cheerful flowers and vibrant colors (right).

VIBRANT

Never neglect color. It plays an important

THE COLOR of both food and tableware affects our enjoyment of meals more than we might imagine: vibrant colors set our taste buds tingling. Entertain colorfully, and your meals will always be memorable.

Phlox

Ranunculus

Rose

Selaginella

FLOATING FLOWERS

Place shallow bowls of floating, brightly colored flowers on the table where they will not interrupt your view. Choose flowers and foliage in vivid colors that contrast and clash excitingly. Here, I have used ferny selaginella and roses in an etched, black glass bowl.

CONTRAST
Note how much the effect changes when flowers of different colors are used. Try alternative varieties to tie in with your own setting.

1 Trim off the leafy stems, leaving about ½ in (1 cm). If necessary, make small bunches by tying 3–4 stems together.

2 Cut each of the flower stems just below the base of its flowerhead. Be careful not to dislodge the petals.

3 Fill a shallow bowl with water. Place foliage bunches in first, then position your flowers (above left).

part in the enjoyment of food

FLOWER SETTINGS
Small bowls with roses, gerbera, and fern leaves are arranged at each place setting to echo the main display.

BOLD NAPKINS
When tied in a bow with pink wire-edged ribbon, blue linen napkins are brightened even more.

PATTERNED TABLECLOTH
As demonstrated by the faux tapestry cloth that sets the color theme for the china, tablecloths need not always form a neutral backdrop.

SEASCAPE

Nothing sharpens the appetite more than

VISUALIZE SAILS on a glittering sea and whitewashed houses in the sun. Then create this sparkling atmosphere using the sunbleached hues borrowed from land and seascapes.

PAPER-RIBBON NAPKIN RINGS
Follow through the seaside theme by making napkin rings in sea-green pleated paper ribbon.

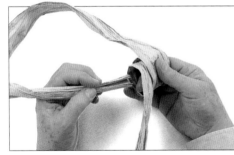

1 Cut a 39in (1m) length of paper ribbon for each person. Wind the ribbon twice around two fingers (this loop will hold the napkin). Thread one end through the loop.

2 The two ends should be roughly equal in length. Keeping two fingers in the loop to preserve its shape, tie a simple up-and-over knot with the ends.

3 Thread one end between the knot and the loop and pull tight. Fan out and straighten the knot. Choose a neat diagonal or a V-shaped cut, and trim the ends to the required length.

Trim ends in preferred shape

a walk beside the sea

VEGETABLE POT
Fill a small terra-cotta pot with Spanish moss and nestle a vegetable, such as miniature broccoli or the cauliflower seen here, on top.

SHELL SALT CELLAR
Use a seashell as a receptacle for coarse sea salt. Mussel shells lined with mother-of-pearl would be suitable, too.

GLASSES
Frosted glasses harmonize perfectly with the muted colors of the tableware.

DECORATIVE VEGETABLE DISPLAY

Vegetables and foliage nestling in a simple painted box make an eyecatching and original decoration for the center of the dining table or a side table. Bleached whites associate with dusty blues, sea greens, and washed wood tones, to continue our seascape theme (pages 48–9); from the huge selection that is available, choose vegetables to match your color scheme.

Cauliflower

1 ◁ Use a shallow box, here a wooden seed tray, and line it, if necessary, with a protective sheet of plastic. Loosely fill the box with attractive foliage such as eucalyptus.

2 ▷ Position the large vegetables first. The canteloupe, apples, cauliflower, white radishes, and artichokes form the framework that supports smaller items.

Corn

SEED BOX
Paint a simple wooden seed tray with a single coat, in a color that suits your theme.

3 ◁ Add any smaller vegetables, such as garlic and mushrooms, before inserting sea holly and wheat spikes to give balance and texture to the overall display (right).

Russet apple

Artichoke

Canteloupe

Garlic

White radish

Eucalyptus

TEXTURE & CONTRAST
*The dominant rounded
forms of large vegetables are
offset by contrasting spikes
of wheat and sea holly, and
airy eucalyptus flowers.*

Mushroom

Sea holly

51

MENUS
There is no greater luxury than lingering

ALFRESCO LUNCH

Here's a combination of simple flavors that spell out summer sunshine. Each of the courses is quick to prepare. *Serves 6*

FIG & FETA SALAD
This impressive dish is light, easy to make, and a glorious feast for both the eye and palate.

FRESH SAUTÉED SARDINES
You will be transported to a cool vine-covered courtyard on the edge of the glittering sea with this zesty mix of fish and herbs.

AROMATIC FRUIT SALAD
Finish off with a taste of the sun in the form of these exotic fruit-packed parchment bundles.

DRINKS
Enjoy the aromatic crispness of a white Rioja with this summer menu.

PLANNING NOTES
The aromatic fruit salad can be arranged, ready for baking, well in advance of the meal. Bear in mind that preparing parchment bundles for more than 12 can take time. The fig and feta salad can be made in quantity up to a couple of hours in advance. Prepare the sauce for the sardines up to 12 hours before you need it, but cook the fish at the last moment. *See pages 54–5 for recipes.*

FLAVORS OF ASIA

This menu is characterized by the sharp spicy flavors that typify Eastern cuisine. *Serves 6*

SHRIMP SOUP
Once you taste this soup, you'll recognize that shrimp and coconut are made for each other.

ORIENTAL BUNDLES WITH SPICY SAUCE
Crispy phyllo bundles of thinly sliced pork and crunchy cashews, complemented by a tangy sauce.

GINGER SORBET
Being sweet vegetables, carrots work well in this exotic ice with ginger. The sorbet is temptingly served in edible ginger baskets.

DRINKS
Sake offered warm is the ideal accompaniment. Have jasmine tea as a nonalcoholic alternative.

PLANNING NOTES
Make the ginger sorbet up to six weeks in advance – it's a great standby for unexpected visitors. The ginger baskets will keep in an airtight tin for up to two weeks. Although the bundles take some time to assemble, the shrimp soup and ginger sorbet are simplicity itself to make. The bundles are best cooked and eaten immediately, so can be unsuitable for large numbers. *See pages 56–7 for recipes.*

over a lazy lunch

WINTER FARE

❧

The food we enjoy varies with the seasons.
Winter is a time for hearty dishes. This is a menu of
satisfying and sophisticated cold-weather treats.
Serves 12

POTATO & BACON SALAD
*Add tiny quantites of truffles to this salad to make it extra
special; potatoes are superb at taking on their flavor.*

PEPPERED LAMB
*Pepper enlivens the taste buds and enhances the flavor of the
tender, sweet meat.*

WINTER COMPOTE WITH PRUNE ICE CREAM
*Dried fruits have an intensity of flavor that is just right in
the depths of winter. This medley is delicious served with
prune ice cream.*

DRINKS
The softness of red Merlot wine makes it ideal for this lunch.

PLANNING NOTES
The ice cream can be made up to six weeks in advance.
Make the compote two days ahead, since it improves over
time. Prepare the potato and bacon salad the day before,
especially if using truffles, to allow the flavors to develop;
arrange it on salad greens at the last minute. The sauce for
the peppered lamb can also be made a day ahead, if necessary;
keep it covered in the refrigerator. The lamb is best eaten
immediately after cooking; always use the finest-quality meat.
See pages 58–9 for recipes.

SEASIDE FAVORITES

❧

The association with sparkling seas and
whitewashed clapboard houses makes these
dishes irresistible. *Serves 6*

FISH CAKES WITH HERB SAUCE
*No heaviness here: just wonderful fresh fish with mayonnaise
and herbs, fried to crisp perfection and accompanied by a
delicate herb sauce.*

BLUEBERRY TART
*The family recipe of my friend Mary Lublin combines cooked
and raw blueberries in a sharp, not-too-sweet sauce. The fruit
explodes with flavor as you eat it.*

DRINKS
*Iced tea, a refreshing favorite specialty, is an ideal choice,
served with or without lemon.*

PLANNING NOTES
The pastry case for the blueberry tart can be made two days
in advance and stored in an airtight container. For the fish
cakes, prepare the fish mixture and sauce several hours ahead
of the meal and keep refrigerated. The fish cakes can be fried
up to one hour before serving, if you keep them warm.
See pages 60–1 for recipes.

ALFRESCO LUNCH FOR 6

FIG & FETA SALAD
20 MINUTES

INGREDIENTS
3 LARGE TOMATOES (PREFERABLY BEEFSTEAK)
6OZ (175G) FETA CHEESE, CRUMBLED
6 SPRIGS BASIL, FINELY CHOPPED
¾ CUP (90G) BLACK OLIVES, PITTED
8 FIGS
2 ZUCCHINIS
2 TBSP BALSAMIC VINEGAR, PLUS
EXTRA TO SERVE
SALT & PEPPER TO TASTE
WATERCRESS TO GARNISH

1 Peel and quarter the tomatoes, remove and discard the cores and seeds, and finely chop the flesh. Place in a salad bowl with the feta, basil, and olives. Dice 6 of the figs and add them to the bowl.

2 Cut the zucchinis in half and shave them lengthwise into thin ribbon strips, using a vegetable peeler. Roll 18 strips into tight cylinders and set aside. Finely chop the remaining strips and add to the bowl.

3 Add the vinegar and seasoning to the salad and toss well. Cover and refrigerate until required (preferably no longer than 4 hours).

4 Just before serving, place a plain round cookie cutter – about 3½in (9cm) in diameter – on a serving plate. Pile the salad into the center of the cutter and press down lightly. Remove the cutter carefully and repeat for the remaining servings.

5 Slice the remaining figs and serve with the salad. Arrange 3 reserved zucchini rolls on top of each salad, garnish with watercress, and sprinkle over a little balsamic vinegar.

COOK'S TIPS
The salad can be varied according to the season. Always use brightly colored ingredients; cut them finely so they hold together in the mold.

FRESH SAUTÉED SARDINES
10 MINUTES   10 MINUTES   30 MINUTES SOAKING

INGREDIENTS
¼ CUP (60G) RAISINS
18 FRESH SARDINES
5 TBSP (75G) ALL-PURPOSE FLOUR
SALT & PEPPER TO TASTE
3 TBSP OLIVE OIL
3 GARLIC CLOVES, SKINS LEFT ON, CRUSHED
UNDER THE FLAT OF A KNIFE
6 SHALLOTS, FINELY CHOPPED
3 BAY LEAVES
½ CUP (125ML) RED WINE VINEGAR
4 TBSP PINE NUTS, LIGHTLY TOASTED
SALAD GREENS & FOCACCIA (SEE
PAGE 186) TO SERVE

1 Soak the raisins in water for 30 minutes. Gut and scale the sardines, if necessary, and remove their heads. Toss lightly in seasoned flour.

2 Heat the olive oil in a large frying pan. Add the garlic and sardines and sauté gently for about 1½ minutes each side. Transfer the sardines to a warmed dish to keep hot in the oven.

3 To make the sauce, add the shallots and bay leaves to the same pan and cook over medium heat until the

shallots are just softened. Add the vinegar, pine nuts, and raisins and cook until bubbling. Discard the garlic.

4 To serve, arrange the sardines on a bed of mixed salad greens and pour the hot sauce over them. Serve with homemade Focaccia.

COOK'S TIP
These sardines are also delicious cooked for the same length of time on the barbecue, but be sure not to overcook them.

FRESH SAUTÉED
SARDINES

AROMATIC FRUIT SALAD

20 MINUTES　10 MINUTES

INGREDIENTS
1 LARGE RIPE MANGO, PEELED
1 LARGE PINEAPPLE, PEELED
3 PASSION FRUITS (OPTIONAL)
2 LIMES, JUICE & GRATED ZEST
6 SHAKES OF ANGOSTURA BITTERS
6 PINCHES EACH OF GROUND CLOVES, ALLSPICE,
& BLACK PEPPER
4 TBSP SOFT DARK BROWN SUGAR
6 TBSP (90ML) DARK RUM (OPTIONAL)

1 Preheat oven to 400°F/200°C. Cut the mango and pineapple flesh into chunks. Halve the passion fruits, if using, and scoop out their flesh together with the seeds.

2 Cut 6 pieces of baking parchment, 12in (30cm) square. Fold each square diagonally. Open out and lay 1 piece of parchment on a plate. Place one-sixth of the fruit on one side of the fold. Sprinkle a dash of the lime juice and zest, the bitters, and a pinch of

each of the spices. Add 2 teaspoons of sugar and 1 tablespoon of rum, if using.

3 Fold the baking parchment over the fruits to enclose, then double-fold the edges. Pleat the folded edges of the triangle. Place on a baking sheet. Repeat to make 5 more bundles.

4 Bake in the oven for 10 minutes. Serve the unopened bundles with fruit sorbet or ice cream, allowing your guests to tear them open at the table.

FLAVORS OF ASIA FOR 6

SHRIMP SOUP

🥄 15 MINUTES 🍲 15 MINUTES

INGREDIENTS

12–18 RAW JUMBO SHRIMP, ABOUT 8OZ (250G)
1⅔ CUPS (400ML) WATER
1⅔ CUPS (400ML) COCONUT MILK
1 TBSP FISH SAUCE
2 TSP SUGAR
1½ LIMES, JUICE & GRATED ZEST
3 FRESH GREEN CHILIES, SEEDED
& FINELY CHOPPED
3 STALKS LEMONGRASS, FINELY CHOPPED
2 GARLIC CLOVES, CRUSHED
1IN (2.5CM) PIECE OF GALANGAL,
PEELED & THINLY SLICED
6 KAFFIR LIME LEAVES (PREFERABLY
FRESH), TORN
1½ TBSP TAMARIND PULP (OPTIONAL)
⅓ – ½ CUCUMBER, CUT IN MATCHSTICKS
3 TBSP FRESH CILANTRO, COARSELY
CHOPPED TO GARNISH

1 Prepare the shrimp (see Step 1, page 94). Place the shells in a large saucepan with the water, coconut milk, fish sauce, sugar, lime juice, and chilies. Bring to a boil and simmer for 5 minutes. Strain and discard the shrimp shells, returning the cooking liquid to the saucepan.

2 Add the lemongrass, garlic, galangal, lime leaves, lime zest, and tamarind, if using, and return to a boil. Simmer for 5 minutes.

3 Add the cucumber and shrimp and cook for 2 more minutes. Serve in warmed soup bowls, and sprinkle with the cilantro.

COOK'S TIPS

Galangal, kaffir lime leaves, and tamarind pulp are all available in Oriental grocery stores. Galangal can be replaced with a ½in (1cm) piece of fresh ginger, peeled and very finely chopped. Use the grated zest of 2 limes instead of kaffir lime leaves, if necessary.

SHRIMP SOUP

ORIENTAL BUNDLES WITH SPICY SAUCE

30 Minutes   18 Minutes   1 Hour Marinating

INGREDIENTS

1 TBSP FISH SAUCE
6 TBSP (90ML) OYSTER SAUCE
3 TBSP LIGHT SOY SAUCE
3 FRESH RED CHILIES, SEEDED
& FINELY CHOPPED
5 GARLIC CLOVES, FINELY CHOPPED
1IN (2.5CM) PIECE FRESH GINGER,
PEELED & FINELY CHOPPED
½ LB (225G) PORK FILLET, WELL CHILLED
2 TSP VEGETABLE OIL
4 SHALLOTS, FINELY CHOPPED
1 CUP (125G) UNSALTED CASHEW NUTS,
COARSELY CHOPPED
24 SHEETS PHYLLO DOUGH, APPROXIMATELY
12 X 7IN (30 X 17CM), ABOUT 8OZ (250G)
6 TBSP (90G) BUTTER, MELTED
2 TBSP SESAME OIL
½ TSP GROUND CINNAMON
¼ TSP GROUND NUTMEG
2 TSP GROUND CORIANDER
½ CUP (125ML) WATER
2 TBSP SHERRY OR CIDER VINEGAR
1 LIME, JUICE & GRATED ZEST
2 TSP SUGAR

1 To make the marinade, combine the fish sauce, 3 tablespoons of the oyster sauce, 1 tablespoon of the soy sauce, 2 chilies, 2 garlic cloves, and the ginger. Cut the pork into very thin slices and place in a shallow non-metallic dish. Pour over the marinade, cover, and let marinate in the refrigerator for 1 hour.

2 Heat the vegetable oil in a wok or frying pan and stirfry the shallots until pale golden. Add the pork with the marinade, and the nuts, and continue to fry until the pork is golden. Let cool.

3 Preheat oven to 350°F/180°C. Lay out 1 sheet of phyllo dough, brush lightly with melted butter, lay a second sheet crosswise over it, and brush this with butter. Turn the pastry over. Place about a tablespoon of the pork and nut mixture in the center.

4 Gather up the pastry around the meat, twist into a bundle, and place it on a greased baking sheet. Make 11 more bundles in this way. Bake for about 15–18 minutes, until golden.

5 Meanwhile, make the spicy sauce. Heat the sesame oil in a small pan. Add the remaining garlic and the cinnamon, nutmeg, and coriander, and brown lightly.

6 Remove the pan from the heat and add the water, remaining soy sauce, oyster sauce, vinegar, lime juice and zest, and sugar. Stir. Return to a boil and simmer for 4–5 minutes. Serve the Oriental bundles with the sauce drizzled over, accompanied by snow peas and baby asparagus.

COOK'S TIP

For an attractive presentation, tie the top of the bundles with 2 strands of chives before baking.

GINGER SORBET

15 Minutes   10 Minutes   8 Hours Chilling

INGREDIENTS

1¼ CUPS (300ML) WATER
1¼ CUPS (300G) SUGAR
2 CUPS (500ML) CARROT JUICE
2 LIMES, JUICE & GRATED ZEST
2–3IN (5–7½ CM) PIECE OF FRESH GINGER,
PEELED & FINELY CHOPPED
1 EGG, WHITE ONLY
12 GINGER BASKETS (SEE BRANDY SNAPS
COOK'S TIP, PAGE 180)

1 Heat the water and sugar in a saucepan over moderate heat. Bring to a boil, stirring until the syrup has dissolved and is clear. Add the carrot juice, lime juice and zest, and ginger. Let cool, then refrigerate for 2 hours, until chilled.

2 Pour the mixture into a freezer-proof container, cover, and freeze for 3 hours, stirring at the end of each hour. On the final stirring, lightly beat the egg white, then fold it into the mixture. Refreeze for at least 3 hours.

3 Transfer the sorbet to the refrigerator 30 minutes before serving, to soften. Allow 2 scoops per person and serve in Ginger Baskets.

COOK'S TIPS

If you have an ice cream maker, follow the manufacturer's instructions. Avoid serving foods containing raw egg to children and the elderly.

WINTER FARE FOR 12

POTATO & BACON SALAD
— 15 MINUTES · 15 MINUTES · 12 HOURS MARINATING —

INGREDIENTS
2 WHITE TRUFFLES, FRESH OR
BOTTLED (OPTIONAL)
2 TBSP OLIVE OIL
¾ LB (350G) SMOKED PANCETTA OR SMOKED
BACON, TRIMMED & SLICED
2½ LB (1.25KG) NEW POTATOES, SCRUBBED
6 SPRIGS FRESH MINT
⅔ CUP (150ML) VINAIGRETTE (SEE PAGE 185)
SALAD GREENS TO SERVE

1 If you are using fresh truffles, peel them the day before and reserve the peel. Keep the truffles wrapped and airtight in refrigerator until required.

2 Heat the oil in a frying pan. Add the bacon with the truffle peel, if using, and cook until golden. Remove the bacon and drain on paper towels. Discard the truffle peel.

3 Cook the potatoes and mint in a large saucepan of salted boiling water for about 12–15 minutes, until the potatoes are just cooked. Drain.

4 When the potatoes are cool enough to handle, cut into ¼ in (½ cm) slices. Place in a large, nonmetallic dish. Sprinkle with the bacon and pour over the Vinaigrette. Cover and marinate overnight in the refrigerator.

5 Slice the truffles very thinly. To serve, arrange the potato and bacon with the Vinaigrette on a bed of salad greens and add the truffle slices.

COOK'S TIP
If you are using bottled truffles, use some of the oil to make the Vinaigrette.

PEPPERED LAMB
— 30 MINUTES · 55 MINUTES —

INGREDIENTS
1 OZ (30G) DRIED CEPES
2 CUPS (500ML) HOT WATER
4 TBSP UNSALTED BUTTER
8 ANCHOVY FILLETS, FINELY CHOPPED
4 TBSP OLIVE OIL
2 BONED & TRIMMED LOINS OF LAMB, ABOUT
2½ LB (1.25KG) EACH, WITH BONES RESERVED
2 GARLIC CLOVES, SKINS LEFT ON, CRUSHED
UNDER THE FLAT OF A KNIFE
3 CUPS (750ML) RED WINE
4 TBSP MIXED PEPPERCORNS, CRUSHED
4 TBSP FRESH MINT, FINELY CHOPPED
TAGLIATELLE & BRAISED ENDIVE (SEE
PAGE 187) TO SERVE

COOK'S TIP
Unless you have a very large pan, you may find you need to cook the lamb in 2 pans.

1 To make the sauce, grind the cepes to a powder in an electric grinder or mortar and soak in the hot water for 30 minutes. Cream the butter and anchovies to a paste and refrigerate.

2 Meanwhile, heat 2 tablespoons of oil in a flameproof casserole. Add the lamb bones and garlic and cook until brown. Gradually add the wine and reduce to about ⅔ cup (150ml) over low heat. Add the mushroom liquid and reduce by half. Discard the bones and garlic and reserve the sauce.

3 To prepare the lamb, brush with 1 tablespoon of oil and roll in the peppercorns mixed with mint. Heat the remaining oil in a large frying pan. Sear each loin all over until charred. Lower the heat and cook for a further 4–8 minutes, turning regularly, until just cooked inside. Transfer to a warmed dish; keep hot in a low oven.

4 To the same pan, add the reserved sauce and bring to a boil. Cut the anchovy butter into small pieces and add them gradually to the sauce, whisking after each addition, until the sauce is smooth.

5 Carve the lamb into ½ in (1cm) slices and serve with the sauce, accompanied by Braised Endive and tagliatelle.

BRAISED
ENDIVE

PEPPERED
LAMB

WINTER COMPOTE WITH PRUNE ICE CREAM

—— 15 MINUTES   20 MINUTES   8 HOURS CHILLING ——

INGREDIENTS
1LB (500G) PRUNES, PITTED
2 CUPS (500ML) PRUNE JUICE
½ CUP (125G) SUGAR
5 LEMONS, JUICE & GRATED ZEST
2½ CUPS (600ML) HEAVY CREAM, CHILLED
6 TBSP (90ML) ARMAGNAC OR BRANDY
1½ CUPS (375ML) PORT
OR MEDIUM DRY SHERRY
10 CLOVES
24 DRIED PEAR HALVES
24 DRIED APRICOTS
12 DRIED FIGS

1 To make the ice cream, heat 10oz (300g) of the prunes, the prune juice, the sugar, and the juice of 3 lemons for about 10 minutes, until the prunes are soft. Purée in a blender, let cool, then refrigerate for at least 2 hours, until thoroughly chilled.

2 Whisk in the cream, grated zest of 3 lemons, and the Armagnac. Turn the mixture into a rigid freezer-proof container, cover, and freeze for 3 hours, stirring at the end of each hour

(follow the manufacturer's instructions if you use an ice cream maker). Refreeze for at least 3 hours.

3 To make the compote, heat the port, cloves, the juice and zest of 2 lemons, and the dried fruits in a small saucepan. Do not allow to boil. Move to a bowl, cover, and refrigerate overnight. Transfer the ice cream to the refrigerator 30 minutes before serving, to soften. Serve the compote with 2 scoops of the ice cream for each person.

59

SEASIDE FAVORITES FOR 6

FISH CAKES WITH
HERB SAUCE

BLUEBERRY
TART

FISH CAKES WITH HERB SAUCE

25 MINUTES 20 MINUTES 1 HOUR CHILLING

INGREDIENTS

1½ LB (750G) SMOKED HADDOCK OR COD
¼ LB (125G) LARGE COOKED SHRIMP
3 TBSP DILL, FINELY CHOPPED, PLUS
SPRIGS TO GARNISH
10 TBSP PARSLEY, FINELY CHOPPED
1 CUP (250ML) CRÈME FRAÎCHE
OR LIGHT SOUR CREAM
4 TBSP MAYONNAISE
SALT & PEPPER TO TASTE
2 TSP DIJON MUSTARD
1 CUP (45G) FRESH WHITE BREAD CRUMBS
2 TBSP UNSALTED BUTTER
2 TBSP VEGETABLE OIL
LEMON WEDGES TO GARNISH

1 To make the fish cakes, place the fish in a saucepan, half cover with water, cover and simmer gently for 5–10 minutes, until tender. Drain and let cool. Flake the fish, discarding the skin and bones.

2 In a food processor, combine the fish, shrimp, half of the dill, half of the parsley, 2 tablespoons of crème fraîche, the mayonnaise, and seasoning. Process for a few seconds, until the mixture is just combined. Cover and refrigerate for 1 hour.

3 Meanwhile, prepare the sauce: in a food processor, combine the remaining dill, parsley, and crème fraîche with the mustard and a little

seasoning, until thickened. Put the mixture in a bowl, cover, and refrigerate until required.

4 Remove the fish cake mixture from the refrigerator. Divide the mixture into 12 round patties, about ¾ in (2cm) in depth. Roll them in bread crumbs.

5 Divide the butter and oil between 2 heavy-bottomed frying pans. Fry the fish cakes for about 10 minutes, turning, until golden on both sides.

6 Serve hot with the chilled sauce and a green salad. Garnish with lemon wedges and dill sprigs.

BLUEBERRY TART

20 MINUTES 30 MINUTES

INGREDIENTS

¾ LB (375G) SWEET SHORTCRUST PASTRY
(SEE PAGE 184)
1½ LB (750G) BLUEBERRIES
1½ LEMONS, JUICE & GRATED ZEST
2 TBSP SUGAR
1 TBSP CORNSTARCH, SIFTED
4 TBSP WATER
CONFECTIONERS' SUGAR TO DUST
CRÈME FRAÎCHE OR WHIPPED CREAM
TO SERVE

1 For the crust, roll out the pastry and press into a 10in (25cm) loose-bottomed fluted tart pan. Prick the bottom of the pastry all over with a fork then refrigerate for 30 minutes.

2 Preheat oven to 350°F/180°C. Line the dough with waxed paper, fill with dried beans, and bake for 15 minutes, until the pastry is just set. Remove the waxed paper and beans. Return to the oven for 15 minutes more until golden. Let cool completely.

3 For the filling, heat half of the blueberries in a saucepan with the lemon juice and zest and sugar. Mix the cornstarch with the water, then add to the blueberry mixture, stirring until

well combined. Bring to a boil, then simmer, covered, for about 5–10 minutes, stirring occasionally, until the fruit is soft.

4 Let the blueberry mixture cool for about 10 minutes, then stir in the remaining berries.

5 Place the pastry shell on a serving plate and fill with the berry mixture. Let cool completely. Dust with confectioners' sugar and serve with a large spoonful of crème fraîche.

COOK'S TIP

The cooked filling can be made with frozen blueberries, but ¾lb (375g) should still be fresh.

DINNER

EVENING HAS TO BE THE OPTIMUM TIME TO ENTERTAIN. WORK AND OTHER DAYTIME ACTIVITIES ARE OVER, PEOPLE ARE ALL READY TO WIND DOWN AND LET THE DAY'S PRESSURES RECEDE. APPETITES ARE SHARP, AND WE LOOK FORWARD TO BEING SOCIABLE. SO SEND OUT INVITATIONS, SELECT A TANTALIZING MENU, ADORN THE DINING TABLE, PREPARE SUMPTUOUS FOOD AND DRINKS, AND JOIN YOUR GUESTS IN STIMULATING CONVERSATION.

*Prepare the Festive Celebration menu (page 74) for a rich and colorful
Carnival party (right) at which you and all your guests wear masks.*

CARNIVAL
Celebration is the elixir of the gods

CARNIVAL IS ALL about merrymaking, mystery, and intrigue, and color always plays a large role. Here I've used black and white, the colors of night and light, to create the atmosphere.

Use eyeglasses to plot position of eyehole

FLOWER BOWL

Place two or three shallow bowls filled with flowers (see page 46 for technique) on the table for decoration. If you have other flower arrangements elsewhere, use some of the same flowers for floating; my choice was inspired by the epergne (pages 66–7).

White dill *Phlox*

Rose

HARLEQUIN MASKS

Simple to make and paint, these are designed to relate to the china. Lay one beside each place.

1 To make a template, plot a center line. Use a plate to draw an oval 8in (20cm) long. Draw a design on one half, cut it out, fold along center, trace other half.

2 Cut out the other side of the template, then use it to trace as many masks as you need onto stiff cardboard. Cut them out. Use a craft knife to make eyeholes.

3 In a well-ventilated area, spray stripes of paint, first in one direction, then in another, to create diamonds. Finally, glue a painted stick to each mask.

Spray stripes between two strips of cardboard

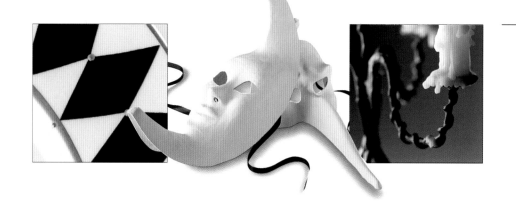

SILVER BOW
Lacelike silver ribbon tied in simple bows adds sparkle to this formal setting.

BLACK STONE TABLE
A dark surface like this stone (or a black tablecloth) forms a dramatic background for white place mats.

FLOWER BOWL
A soup bowl belonging to the same set of dishes makes an excellent showcase for flowers on the table.

GRAND CENTERPIECE

The epergne was a fashionable decoration for the center of a dining table or a sideboard around the turn of the century. It was usually made of glass, often etched, with several tiers to hold a fountain of fruits, flowers, and candies. Here, I have improvised my own epergne with two glass cake stands and a small flared glass vase for a similarly effective display.

Large cake stand

Small cake stand

Small vase

1 Attach a small cake stand onto the center of a larger one using adhesive putty. Secure a vase or fluted glass, filled with water, to the small stand to form a tower.

2 Stick florists' prongs to the cake stands with adhesive putty. Attach small bunches of grapes to each end of several wires, then lay them across the stands.

3 Make sure the prongs are firm and correctly positioned before pushing small blocks of soaked florists' foam onto them; the putty will not adhere to a wet surface.

4 Push leaves and flowers into the foam, starting with larger items on the bottom layer. Work around the arrangement, and then move up to the next tier.

5 Arrange flowers and leaves in the vase at the top. Finally, add grass to create a fountain effect (see main image), and finish by filling in any gaps.

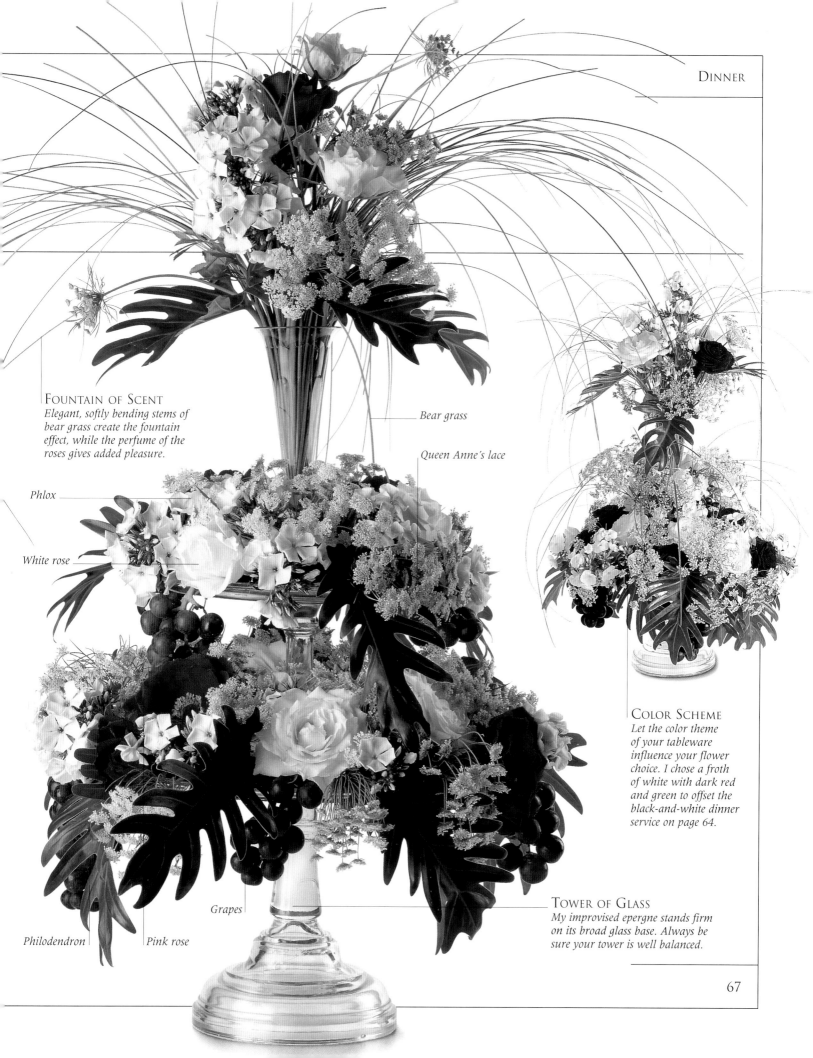

FOUNTAIN OF SCENT
Elegant, softly bending stems of bear grass create the fountain effect, while the perfume of the roses gives added pleasure.

Bear grass

Queen Anne's lace

Phlox

White rose

COLOR SCHEME
Let the color theme of your tableware influence your flower choice. I chose a froth of white with dark red and green to offset the black-and-white dinner service on page 64.

Grapes

TOWER OF GLASS
My improvised epergne stands firm on its broad glass base. Always be sure your tower is well balanced.

Philodendron

Pink rose

67

FIRESIDE

"... intimate delights, fireside enjoyments,

GOOD FOOD in an atmosphere of warmth and comfort gives rise to superb conversation. Lighted candles and a crackling fire ensure an enjoyable supper.

CANDLE BASKET

Flowers, seeds, nuts, and spices mingle with similarly colored candles in this box of delight. Never leave lit candles unattended.

WOODEN TABLE
This rough-hewn wood table is a good foil for the other warm, earthy textures.

1 Line three sections of a cutlery basket with plastic. Place four candles at random, securing with adhesive putty. Tie a bundle of cinnamon with raffia.

2 Cut wet foam slices to fit the plastic-lined sections, slicing curves for the candles where necessary. Fill the unlined sections with pecans and litchis, and position the cinnamon.

3 Push fresh roses and coneflowers, with stems cut to 1in (2.5cm) long, into the wet foam to form a dense cover. Fill in with pecans and litchis, to complete the display (top). Dampen the foam so the flowers last.

home-born happiness."

WILLIAM COWPER 1731–1800

CINNAMON CANDLE

Stand a candle with a cinnamon-stick fence at each place. To make the fence, tie a loop at the middle of a length of string, then tie the sticks on behind. Make a bow through the loop when the fence is long enough.

CUTLERY REST

To encourage informality, use the same cutlery for all the savory dishes. A tripod of cinnamon sticks tied with string forms an attractive resting place for the cutlery between courses.

SPRING
This bright enchanted time of joy reborn

SPRING SKIES, flowers, and young leaves, with their fresh clear colors, give a mouthwatering backdrop to light and delicate meals.

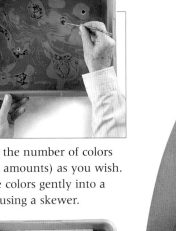

Cut the marbled paper into smaller sections or fold to suit your settings

MARBLED PAPER PLACE CARDS
Make highly individual place names or menu cards by marbling paper in colors to match your setting. Marbling paints are available from craft shops.

1 Half-fill a shallow basin with water and add 3 tablespoons of vinegar. Using a dropper, drip in 6 drops of your first color.

2 Drip in about twice as many drops of your second color, then add a third color on top of each of these drops.

3 Vary the number of colors (and amounts) as you wish. Spin the colors gently into a pattern using a skewer.

4 Take a piece of uncoated, preferably porous paper. Make sure that the whole sheet will fit flat in the basin.

5 Place the paper flat on the water; it will curl almost immediately. Remove, lay face up to dry, and then iron flat.

COLORS OF SPRING
Mixing and matching fresh-colored plates gives the table a springlike appearance.

MARBLED PLACE NAMES
Marbled name cards draw together the elements on the table, echoing the colors of the tableware.

FRESH FLOWERS
Single tulip stems in jars are striking when arranged alongside candles chosen to match the dishes.

A TABLE DISPLAY FOR SPRING

The first flowers of spring cause a *frisson* of excitement, and they simply beg to be displayed. A Turkish miniature inspired this table arrangement of candles with bud vases that show off the waxy beauty of tulips, an archetypal spring flower. Place a single vase beside each place if table space is limited.

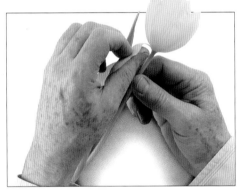

1 Many tulips can be "opened" by furling back their petals to give a lilylike effect. To do this, invert the base of the petal, just above the bottom of the flowerhead.

2 Taking care not to bruise the petals, continue to furl them back, gently easing them out with your fingers. Peel back all petals, including the inner ones.

Double tulip

BUD VASE
Each teardrop-shaped vase in frosted glass holds just one or two tulip stems.

TRAY
A painted wooden tray contains all the vases and candles and provides them with a steady base.

FLOWERS
*Fresh spring yellow, white,
pastel pink, and lime green
illuminate this arrangement
and enhance the table
setting on pages 70–1.*

Single tulip

CANDLES & HOLDERS
*Tulip-shaped glass holders are
most appropriate for the candles,
themselves in spring colors of
pink, green, and yellow.*

**INDIVIDUAL
ARRANGEMENTS**
*If your table is too
small to hold a tray,
two tulip stems in a
bud vase beside each
place setting is just
as decorative.*

73

MENUS 1

"A good dinner and feasting reconciles

FESTIVE CELEBRATION

❧

It's party time. If you cannot be in Rio de Janeiro, Venice, or New Orleans, re-create your own carnival celebrations. Dress up, put on masks, live the part! *Serves 6*

SEARED PEARS & PROSCIUTTO
Pears are an unusual partner for prosciutto; an elegant mix of the simple and the glamorous.

SCALLOPS WITH CHARD
Subtle flavors and textures vie for precedence.

CHOCOLATE TART
A dense, rich treat, this tart will keep the most hardened chocoholic gloriously happy.

DRINKS
Serve a good white Burgundy with the starter and main courses, and a Rhône Muscat, Beaumes-des-Venise, to accompany the chocolate tart.

PLANNING NOTES
Make the chocolate tart a day in advance. Since it is very rich, it is fortunate that you can store any leftovers in the refrigerator for up to four days. The seared pears can also be prepared a day in advance and kept covered and refrigerated, but serve the prosciutto at room temperature. This recipe can easily be scaled up or down depending on the number of guests. Prepare the chard for the main meal an hour or so in advance, and heat it through while the scallops are cooking. *See pages 80–1 for recipes.*

LAVISH PARTY

❧

You will be the toast of the town when you serve this sumptuous menu that is rounded off with a light dessert. *Serves 12*

CRAB TARTLETS WITH LEEK PURÉE
The leek and sherry purée makes an excellent accompaniment to the creamy crab tartlets.

DUCK WITH KUMQUATS
This variation on the traditional orange duck recipe has a tangy sweet-sour sauce made with sliced kumquats.

SUMMER FRUITS WITH CRÈME FRAÎCHE
A glorious summer dessert that is simple and most delicious.

DRINKS
Drink a good lightly chilled Verdicchio with the crab tarts, and a fruity cru Beaujolais such as Brouilly or Fleurie with the duck. Try a Pineau de Charentes with the summer fruits.

PLANNING NOTES
All these dishes can be prepared in part some hours in advance. Make the leek purée, and keep covered and refrigerated prior to serving, then heat it on the stove. Tarts baked earlier the same day can be heated in a moderate oven. Make the kumquat sauce and sear the duck breasts ahead of time, then refrigerate both until needed. Reheat the sauce while the duck is cooking. Prepare the crème fraîche mix and cover the fruits in advance, but grill immediately before eating. *See pages 82–3 for recipes.*

everyone." SAMUEL PEPYS 1663–1703

INTIMATE DINNER

❧

A very special dinner for two, with the luxury of lobster as a main course. *Serves 2*

HERB OMELET WITH CAVIAR
Feather-light with a hint of truffle and a sprinkling of caviar.

LOBSTER WITH ROAST FIGS
The combination of flavors and textures is sublime. This dish also looks wonderful.

ORANGE & GRAPEFRUIT SORBETS
A pair of sorbets with unexpected ingredients.

DRINKS
Vintage Champagne followed by more Champagne. For the non-fizzy-minded, choose a grand or premier cru Chablis as an alternative.

PLANNING NOTES
The sorbets can be made up to six weeks in advance. The sauce for the lobster can be made up to four hours ahead and reheated. Have all the ingredients ready for the omelet, which should be eaten as soon as it is made. The appetizer and main course are best for two people, but the sorbets can be made for more than two batches and used as required.
See pages 84–5 for recipes.

EXOTIC EVENING

❧

All these dishes are subtly spiced to give a well-balanced and exotic menu. *Serves 6*

PEPPERED SCALLOPS
Two colorful sauces accompany the peppery scallops.

LAMB TAGINE WITH COUSCOUS
Tender young lamb stuffed with a piquant-sweet mix of spices, herbs, and prunes.

COCONUT & SAFFRON ICE CREAM
A dreamy, creamy concoction with flavors and textures that are irresistible.

DRINKS
An oaky, buttery New World Chardonnay complements the scallops, and a full, rich, spicy Australian Shiraz, served with the tagine, is ideal. Serve a chilled sweet white port with the ice cream.

PLANNING NOTES
The ice cream can be made up to six weeks ahead. Prepare the stuffing for the lamb tagine in advance, if necessary. The two sauces for the scallops can be prepared ahead of time, kept covered with plastic wrap in the refrigerator, then heated for serving. *See pages 86–7 for recipes.*

MENUS 2

"Woe to the cook whose sauce has no sting."

SPRING DINNER

Fresh, clean flavors of spring are captured in this irresistible menu. *Serves 6*

ARUGULA SOUP
Wonderful arugula is at its sweetest, tangiest best in spring.

TARRAGON CHICKEN
Here, grilled chicken breasts are laced with a tempting tarragon sauce.

LIME & MINT MOLD
A cool, fragrant end to a dinner, which looks beautiful, too.

DRINKS
A lightly oaked Chardonnay would be a perfect accompaniment to this menu. End with a faintly sweet Gewürztraminer.

PLANNING NOTES
The lime and mint mold can be prepared up to two days in advance and kept in the refrigerator. Make the arugula soup up to eight hours ahead. The sauce for the chicken can be prepared up to eight hours in advance, kept covered with plastic wrap in the refrigerator, then reheated gently at the last minute. *See pages 88–9 for recipes.*

SUMMER MENU

The garden is a perfect setting for a summer dinner party. In this menu, the food is light and tantalizingly flavorful. *Serves 6*

BRIE & LENTIL SALAD
The country flavors of this dish are an immediate ticket to sunshine.

TROUT WITH GOOSEBERRY SAUCE
A delicious fish: moist but not oily with a fine, delicate flavor.

STRAWBERRY TART
This tart is most special when made with wild strawberries.

DRINKS
Serve a premier cru Chablis or a Puligny-Montrachet with this menu. If you can find the wild strawberry wine Fragolini, a glass of it would be nectar with the tart.

PLANNING NOTES
The pastry shell for the strawberry tart can be made two days in advance and stored in an airtight tin. Prepare the lentils for the salad up to 24 hours ahead. The gooseberry sauce can also be made 24 hours in advance, covered with plastic wrap in the refrigerator, and then reheated when required. *See pages 90–1 for recipes.*

GEOFFERY CHAUCER C.1340–1400

VEGETARIAN

A scrumptious mix of flavors in a menu that combines taste and texture. *Serves 6*

ROAST TOMATO SOUP
Roasting the tomatoes intensifies their flavor to give an extra fillip to this soup.

BLUE CHEESE SOUFFLÉS
A feather-light, tangy soufflé, juxtaposed with the nutty sweetness of the vegetables.

COFFEE TRUFFLE PUDDINGS
A dessert with a small surprise at its heart.

DRINKS
A full-bodied Rhône rosé wine such as a Tavel or Lirac will go happily with the soup and complement the eggs and cheese of the soufflé. A Gewürztraminer would ideally complement the rich dessert.

PLANNING NOTES
The roast tomato soup can be made 24 hours in advance. Don't be daunted by soufflés; these work every time. Just make sure your guests are ready to receive them as they come out of the oven. *See pages 92–3 for recipes.*

FRUITS OF THE SEA

Choose the freshest of ingredients for this delectable dinner. *Serves 6*

SHRIMP IN HARD CIDER
The sweetness of the shrimp and the dryness of the cider make them a well-matched pair.

TUNA STEAKS WITH RHUBARB
Rhubarb's sharp taste is a good foil for the robust and rich tuna.

MANGO SYLLABUB & ALMOND COOKIES
An old-fashioned recipe with a distinctive new fruit flavor, delicious served with the cookies.

DRINKS
Drink hard cider or a dry apple juice with the shrimp. Serve a New World Semillon Chardonnay with the tuna, and a sweet Riesling with the dessert.

PLANNING NOTES
The syllabub can be made up to 24 hours in advance. Bake the cookies the day before and store in an airtight tin. Cook the shrimp up to one hour in advance and keep them hot in the oven. The tuna can also be prepared one hour in advance, and kept covered and just warm in a low oven. *See pages 94–5 for recipes.*

MENUS 3

"Of soup and love, the first is the best."

HARVEST SUPPER

Autumn is the perfect time to savor the riches of the harvest at their very freshest. *Serves 6*

WILD MUSHROOM RAGOÛT
A good way to make the most of freshly harvested mushrooms gathered at the grocery store.

PHEASANT & APPLES WITH CALVADOS
The earthy, apple flavor of Calvados gives this traditional Normandy dish its distinctive character.

CHOCOLATE & COFFEE CHEESECAKE
Dark chocolate and coffee make good companions in this wonderful rich cheesecake.

DRINKS
A lightly oaked Chardonnay would have the presence to accompany this meal. Enjoy the dessert with a glass of Madeira.

PLANNING NOTES
The mushroom ragoût can be prepared up to 12 hours in advance, kept covered in the refrigerator, then reheated at the last minute. Cook the pheasant breasts up to two hours ahead of the meal, then keep covered and warm in a low oven. The cheesecake needs at least eight hours to set, and will last for up to one week in the refrigerator. *See pages 96–7 for recipes.*

WINTER DINNER

Serve hearty food to keep the winter cold at bay: a soup scented with saffron, a tender beef stew, and a light, steamed dessert. *Serves 6*

SHRIMP, LEEK & SAFFRON SOUP
A melting soup with a great aroma and delicate flavors.

FLEMISH-STYLE BEEF
Cooking beef in beer with herbs lends it a fragrant, tangy-sweet flavor.

STEAMED CRANBERRY PUDDING
This light dessert is topped with a crown of cranberries and an orange and cranberry sauce.

DRINKS
Follow a white Burgundy with the soup by a mature, smooth, and rich Burgundy Pinot Noir such as a Beaune or Pommard, or a fine Californian Zinfandel. Choose an Australian orange Muscat to round off the meal.

PLANNING NOTES
The beef dish is best cooked up to two days in advance. After cooking (step 4), refrigerate until needed, then reheat in a moderate oven for 30 minutes. The soup can be prepared to the end of step 2, and refrigerated for up to two days. Gently reheat the liquid and add the shrimp and cream. The pudding can be made up to eight hours ahead, then gently reheated in its bowl of simmering water for 15 minutes. Prepare the cranberry sauce in advance, too, then warm just before eating. *See pages 98–9 for recipes.*

ANONYMOUS (SPANISH)

FAMILY GATHERING
✑

It often seems appropriate to serve traditional dishes for family, so here is a menu with soup, roast meat, and a rich dessert. Each course is not quite what you would expect, however! *Serves 12*

ITALIAN CABBAGE SOUP
A hearty soup of cabbage, herbs, and cheese from northern Italy.

SPICY PORK ROAST
Spices, herbs, and rum add a Caribbean touch.

MIRACULOUS BLACKBERRY CAKE
A magnificent monster of a dessert with layers of cake, meringue, cream, and blackberries.

DRINKS
Start with a well-chilled dry sparkling wine such as Proseccodli. Follow it with a good Chianti Classico or Chianti Rufina to match the spicy pork.

PLANNING NOTES
The pork must be marinated for 24 hours. Make the meringue and cake the day before and store in an airtight tin, but assemble the cake just before your guests arrive to prevent the cream and berries from softening the cake tiers. Layer the soup (to the end of step 4) up to eight hours in advance, then pour on the boiling stock at the last moment and heat the soup. *See pages 100–1 for recipes.*

COUNTRY FOOD
✑

For an easy and informal meal, serve an interesting pasta, followed by vegetable kebabs, and a fruit compote. *Serves 6*

ASPARAGUS & HAM FETTUCCINE
Your only worry will be that your guests might eat too much of this delicious pasta appetizer!

VEGETABLE & NUT KEBABS
These kebabs are roasted to perfection with a spicy, piquant peanut sauce.

SPICED QUINCES & EARL GREY SORBET
The quinces, like the tea, are sweetly and delicately perfumed.

DRINKS
Serve a high-quality dry Chenin blanc from South Africa or New Zealand, followed by a lightly sweet Gewürztraminer with the spiced quinces.

PLANNING NOTES
Make the sorbet up to six weeks, and the quinces up to 24 hours, in advance. The vegetables for the pasta will keep for four hours, if covered: cook the pasta, reheat the vegetables, and add them with the cream, cheese, and ham to the pasta at the last moment. Prepare the kebab sauce up to four hours before the meal. The kebabs are best cooked and served in one operation, but the ingredients can be skewered, with a little lemon juice squeezed over them, two hours in advance. *See pages 102–3 for recipes.*

FESTIVE CELEBRATION FOR 6

SEARED PEARS & PROSCIUTTO

20 MINUTES   10 MINUTES

INGREDIENTS

3 PEARS (PREFERABLY COMICE)
2 TBSP OLIVE OIL
2 GARLIC CLOVES, SKIN LEFT ON, CRUSHED
UNDER THE FLAT OF A KNIFE
½ CUP (125ML) BALSAMIC VINEGAR
1 TSP SOFT BROWN SUGAR
18 VERY THIN SLICES OF PROSCIUTTO
MÂCHE OR WATERCRESS LEAVES TO SERVE

1 Peel the pears, cut each one in half, and remove the core. Slice each half into 6 wedge-shaped pieces.

2 Heat the olive oil in a skillet and add the garlic and half of the vinegar. Add the pieces of pear to the pan and brown for about 5 minutes, turning halfway during cooking (the vinegar should become sticky and almost disappear). Remove the pan from the heat. Take out the pears and let them cool.

3 Return the pan containing the juices and garlic to the heat and add the sugar and remaining vinegar. Bring to a boil over high heat. Discard the garlic. Arrange the prosciutto and pears on a bed of mâche and drizzle with the hot sauce.

SCALLOPS WITH CHARD

45 MINUTES   12 MINUTES

INGREDIENTS

12 SWISS CHARD STEMS
½ LEMON, JUICE ONLY
30 SHELLED SEA SCALLOPS, CORAL ATTACHED
SCANT 1 CUP (210G) UNSALTED BUTTER
2 GARLIC CLOVES, SKINS LEFT ON, CRUSHED
UNDER THE FLAT OF A KNIFE
1 CUP (90ML) WHITE VERMOUTH
OR DRY WHITE WINE
SALT & PEPPER TO TASTE

1 Trim the ends of the chard and discard the leaves. Cut the stems into strips and steam for about 10 minutes, until *al dente*. Transfer to a warmed dish, pour over the lemon juice, and keep hot in the oven.

2 While the chard is cooking, rinse the scallops, remove any dark strands, and pat dry with paper towels. Detach the corals and purée in a food processor. Halve the white part of each scallop horizontally to give 2 disks.

3 To make the sauce, heat 12 tbsp (180g) of butter in a skillet. Add the garlic and fry gently until it just begins to brown. Pour in the vermouth, bring to a boil, and simmer for 5 minutes,

until reduced by one-third. Remove from the heat and discard the garlic. Stir in the puréed corals and seasoning. Cover and keep warm.

4 Place the scallops on an oiled baking sheet. Brush with the remaining butter, melted, and sprinkle with salt and pepper on both sides. Heat the broiler to high, then place the baking sheet under the broiler and cook the scallops for 1 minute on each side. Serve on a bed of chard, drizzled with the sauce.

COOK'S TIP

You may have to cook the scallops in 2 batches. Keep them hot in a warmed, covered dish in the oven until ready to serve.

CHOCOLATE TART

— 25 MINUTES 35 MINUTES 3 HOURS CHILLING —

INGREDIENTS

¾ LB (375G) SWEET SHORTCRUST PASTRY (SEE
PAGE 184)
12OZ (375G) BITTERSWEET CHOCOLATE
4 TBSP INSTANT COFFEE GRANULES
3 TBSP BRANDY (OPTIONAL)
3¾ CUPS (900ML) HEAVY CREAM
COCOA POWDER & CONFECTIONERS' SUGAR,
SIFTED, TO DECORATE
LIGHT CREAM TO SERVE

COOK'S TIP

This tart is very rich, so serve thin slices. Any
leftovers can be kept in an airtight container in
the refrigerator for up to 4 days.

1 Roll out the pastry and press into a
10in (25cm) loose-bottomed fluted
tart pan. Prick the pastry with a fork
then refrigerate for 30 minutes.

2 Preheat oven to 350°F/180°C. Line
the dough with waxed paper, fill
with dried beans, and bake for 15
minutes until the pastry is just set.
Remove the waxed paper and beans.
Return to the oven for 15 minutes
more, until the pastry is crisp and
golden. Let cool.

3 For the filling, break the chocolate
into small pieces, then heat with the
coffee in a double boiler, or a heatproof
bowl over a pan of simmering water, or
microwave, until just melted. Stir gently
until smooth, but do not beat. Let cool,
then stir in the brandy, if using.

4 Whip the cream until it forms soft
peaks, then gently fold in the
chocolate mixture. Pour into the pastry
shell. Refrigerate for at least 3 hours.

5 To decorate, remove the tart from
the pan and, using 2 strips of
cardboard, make a pattern on the
surface with cocoa and confectioners'
sugar. Serve with light cream.

CHOCOLATE
TART

LAVISH PARTY FOR 12

CRAB TARTLETS WITH LEEK PURÉE

🥄 30 MINUTES 🍲 45 MINUTES

INGREDIENTS

SHORTCRUST PASTRY (SEE PAGE 184)
1½ CUPS (350ML) CRÈME FRAÎCHE
1 LEMON, GRATED ZEST ONLY
2 EGGS, YOLKS ONLY
¾ LB (375G) CRABMEAT
½ TSP GROUND NUTMEG
5 LEEKS (WHITE PART ONLY), FINELY CHOPPED
4 TBSP BUTTER
1 TSP SUGAR
1 TBSP DRY SHERRY
SALAD GREENS TO SERVE

1 For the crust, roll out the pastry and press into twelve 4in (10cm) round fluted tart pans. Prick the bottom of the pastry all over with a fork, then refrigerate for 30 minutes.

2 Preheat oven to 400°F/200°C. Line the dough with waxed paper, fill with dried beans, and bake for 15 minutes. Remove the waxed paper and beans. Let cool.

3 To make the filling, beat the crème fraîche, lemon zest, and egg yolks in a mixing bowl until well mixed, then stir in the crabmeat.

4 Spoon the filling into the pastry cases and sprinkle a pinch of nutmeg over each tartlet. Bake for 15 minutes, until golden.

5 To make the purée, place the leeks in a saucepan with the butter, sugar, and sherry, bring to boil, cover, and simmer for 10 minutes, until soft, then blend in a food processor. Serve the tartlets warm with 2 tablespoons of warm purée per person and a garnish of salad greens.

CRAB TARTLETS WITH LEEK PURÉE

DUCK WITH KUMQUATS

🥄 30 MINUTES 🍲 35 MINUTES

INGREDIENTS
8 DUCK BREASTS, SKINS LEFT ON
2 TSP SUPERFINE SUGAR
2 TBSP OLIVE OIL
2 GARLIC CLOVES, SKINS LEFT ON, CRUSHED
UNDER THE FLAT OF A KNIFE
¾ LB (350G) KUMQUATS
½ CUP (125ML) ORANGE LIQUEUR (PREFERABLY
COINTREAU) OR 2 TBSP HONEY
2¼ CUPS (575ML) RED WINE
2¼ CUPS (575ML) ORANGE JUICE
HERBY POTATOES (SEE PAGE 186) & ROAST
SHALLOTS (SEE PAGE 187) TO SERVE

1 Preheat oven to 400°F/200°C. Make diagonal slits in the skin of the duck breasts to create a lattice effect. Sprinkle the sugar on both sides.

2 Heat the olive oil in a large skillet over high heat. Add the garlic, then 4 of the duck breasts, skin side down. Cook for 3 minutes on each side until they are rich brown, almost burned. Repeat with the remaining duck breasts, reserving the cooking juices and oil for the sauce in the pan.

3 Place all the breasts on a rack over a foil-lined roasting pan and bake in the oven for 18 minutes (the duck should remain pink inside).

4 Meanwhile, make the sauce. Slice each kumquat into 4 rounds and remove the seeds. Remove all but 2 tablespoons of the fat from the skillet and reserve the browned bits and garlic cloves. Return the skillet to moderate heat.

5 Add the kumquats to the pan. Pour in the orange liqueur and light it carefully (if using honey, do not flambé). When the flames have died, stir in the wine, scraping all the browned bits from the sides of the pan. Bring to a boil and reduce the liquid to about 4 tablespoons. Add the orange juice and reduce by half, stirring occasionally. Discard the garlic.

6 Slice each duck breast, and divide between the plates, allowing three-quarters of a breast for each person. Pour the sauce over the meat, and serve with Herby Potatoes, Roast Shallots, and salad greens.

COOK'S TIP
If cooking for 6, use 4 breasts, and halve the remaining ingredients.

SUMMER FRUITS WITH CRÈME FRAÎCHE

🥄 10 MINUTES 🍲 5 MINUTES

INGREDIENTS
½ LB (250G) STRAWBERRIES
(PREFERABLY WILD)
½ LB (250G) RASPBERRIES
½ LB (250G) CHERRIES, PITTED
2 CUPS (500ML) CRÈME FRAÎCHE
3 EGGS, YOLKS ONLY
½ CUP (125G) SUPERFINE SUGAR
3 TBSP ROSE WATER

1 Combine the strawberries, raspberries, and cherries, and spread them over the bottom of a large, shallow ovenproof dish.

2 Preheat the broiler to high. Reserve 2 tablespoons of the sugar. In a large mixing bowl, whisk together the crème fraîche, egg yolks, the remaining sugar, and the rose water until smooth. Pour the cream mixture over the fruit.

3 Sprinkle the reserved sugar over the surface and place the dish under the broiler for about 5 minutes, until the top just begins to brown. Serve immediately.

COOK'S TIP
Make certain that you use a heat-resistant dish as the broiler must be extremely hot.

INTIMATE DINNER FOR 2

HERB OMELET WITH CAVIAR

—— 10 MINUTES —— 8 MINUTES ——

INGREDIENTS
4 LARGE EGGS, SEPARATED
4 TBSP FINELY CHOPPED FRESH PARSLEY,
PLUS SPRIGS TO GARNISH
2 TBSP HEAVY CREAM
SALT & PEPPER TO TASTE
2 TBSP BUTTER
1 TBSP OLIVE OIL
2 TBSP CAVIAR OR LUMPFISH ROE

1 Mix the egg yolks with the chopped parsley, cream, and seasoning.

2 In a mixing bowl, whisk the egg whites until they form stiff peaks. Fold the egg yolk mixture into the whites.

3 Heat the broiler to high. Divide the butter and oil between two 8in (20cm) omelet pans and heat until the butter just begins to brown. Add half of the egg mixture to each pan and turn the heat to low. Cook for 4 minutes.

4 Place the omelets in their pans under the broiler and cook for 3–4 minutes until golden and risen.

5 Place one tablespoon of caviar in the center of each omelet, spread along the center and fold in half. Garnish with the parsley sprigs and serve immediately.

COOK'S TIP
This dish must be cooked and eaten immediately, so make sure you and your guest are ready.

LOBSTER WITH ROAST FIGS

—— 15 MINUTES —— 25 MINUTES ——

INGREDIENTS
4 FIGS
¾ CUP (175G) UNSALTED BUTTER,
CHILLED & IN PIECES
2 TSP BALSAMIC VINEGAR
2 x 1½ LB (2 x 750G) LIVE LOBSTERS
3 TBSP OLIVE OIL
2 TBSP SHERRY VINEGAR
2 TBSP WATER
1 FINELY CHOPPED SHALLOT
1 TBSP FINELY CHOPPED FRESH DILL
SALT & PEPPER TO TASTE
SALAD GREENS & WALNUT DRESSING (SEE
PAGE 185) TO SERVE

COOK'S TIP
To cut the lobsters open, use a very sharp, serrated knife. Remove and discard the dark, threadlike membrane that runs down the length of the lobster before serving.

1 Preheat oven to 450°F/230°C. Remove the tips of the figs, and make 2 cuts at right angles to about three-quarters of the way down. Ease them open and place 1 teaspoon of butter and ½ teaspoon of balsamic vinegar into the centers. Set aside.

2 Next, plunge the lobsters into a large saucepan of boiling water, then immediately remove them. Brush all over with oil, then place them in a roasting pan in the oven.

3 After 8 minutes of cooking, add the figs to the roasting pan containing the lobsters. Bake for 10 minutes longer. While the lobsters and figs are cooking, make the sauce.

4 Heat the sherry vinegar, water, shallot, dill, and seasoning in a small saucepan. Cook gently for 5 minutes, until the shallot has softened and the liquid has almost disappeared.

5 Over low to medium heat, beat in the remaining butter, one piece at a time, whisking between additions until all the butter has been used and the sauce is rich and creamy. Pour it into a sauceboat, cover with plastic wrap, and keep warm.

6 Cut the lobsters in half lengthwise and discard the heads. Arrange the bodies and claws on a bed of salad with Walnut Dressing. Serve with the roast figs and lastly, pour on the sauce.

LOBSTER
WITH
ROAST FIGS

ORANGE & GRAPEFRUIT SORBETS

🥄 25 MINUTES   🍲 20 MINUTES   ⬜ 8 HOURS CHILLING

INGREDIENTS

2½ CUPS (600ML) WATER
2½ CUPS (625G) SUGAR
12 BLOOD ORANGES, JUICE ONLY, CHILLED
2 TSP ANGOSTURA BITTERS
2 LARGE EGGS, WHITES ONLY
3 PINK GRAPEFRUIT, JUICE ONLY, CHILLED
2 TBSP OUZO
FRESH MINT LEAVES TO DECORATE

1 For the orange sorbet, heat half each of the water and sugar in a saucepan. Bring to a boil, stirring until the sugar has dissolved. Add the orange juice and bitters.

2 Make the grapefruit sorbet in the same way, using grapefruit and ouzo instead of oranges and angostura bitters. Let both mixtures cool, then refrigerate for at least 2 hours, until thoroughly chilled.

3 Pour the mixtures into two rigid freezerproof containers, cover, and freeze for 3 hours, stirring both at the end of each hour. On the final stirring, lightly beat the egg whites and stir them into the sorbets. Return to the freezer for at least 3 hours.

4 Transfer the containers to the refrigerator 30 minutes before serving to soften the sorbets. Serve decorated with fresh mint leaves.

EXOTIC EVENING FOR 6

PEPPERED SCALLOPS

🥄 35 MINUTES 🍲 35 MINUTES

INGREDIENTS
1¾ CUPS (475ML) HEAVY CREAM
½ YELLOW PEPPER, SEEDED & THINLY SLICED
½ RED PEPPER, SEEDED & THINLY SLICED
1 TBSP PAPRIKA
½ LEMON, JUICE & GRATED ZEST
SALT TO TASTE
18 SEA SCALLOPS
2 TBSP MILD WHOLE-GRAIN MUSTARD
3 TBSP PINK PEPPERCORNS, CRUSHED
2 TBSP UNSALTED BUTTER
2 TBSP OLIVE OIL
SALAD GREENS & SAFFRON RICE (SEE
PAGE 187) TO SERVE

COOK'S TIP
Scallops are a great delicacy, ideal for an intimate gathering, but bear in mind that they are very costly if you are entertaining on a larger scale.

1 To make the sauces, divide the cream between 2 small saucepans. Add the yellow pepper to one, the red pepper and paprika to the other.

2 Bring them to a boil, cover, then simmer gently for 15 minutes. Allow to cool. Stir the lemon juice and zest into the yellow pepper mixture,

then purée each sauce separately in a blender until smooth. Season to taste.

3 Remove and discard the corals and any dark strands from the scallops. Pat dry with paper towels. Coat them in mustard, then dip them in the crushed peppercorns.

4 In a large skillet, heat the butter and olive oil until the butter just begins to brown. Sauté the scallops in a single layer for about 3 minutes, turning halfway through cooking, until golden and just cooked.

5 Serve immediately, on a bed of greens, with Saffron Rice and 2 tablespoons of each sauce per person.

LAMB TAGINE
WITH
COUSCOUS

LIME & MINT MOLD

1 HOUR   5 MINUTES   3 HOURS CHILLING

INGREDIENTS

1½ CUPS (375ML) SWEET WHITE WINE
3 LIMES, JUICE OF 3 & GRATED ZEST OF 2
3 TBSP SUPERFINE SUGAR
2 TBSP FRESH MINT, FINELY CHOPPED, PLUS
WHOLE MINT LEAVES TO DECORATE
2 TBSP GELATIN
2¼ CUPS (600ML) LIGHT CREAM
1 CUP (175G) RASPBERRIES OR OTHER SOFT
FRUITS
2 TBSP CONFECTIONERS' SUGAR, SIFTED

COOK'S TIPS

Use vegetarian gelatin if you prefer.
Leaf gelatin can also be used instead
of the powdered type; 1oz (30g) will
set this mold, or follow the
instructions on the package.

1 To make the gelatin, heat the wine (reserve 4 tablespoons for the gelatin), juice and zest of 2 limes, superfine sugar, and mint in a saucepan. Bring the mixture almost to a boil, then remove from the heat.

2 In a small saucepan, sprinkle the gelatin over the reserved wine and let it soak for 5 minutes. Place over very low heat and stir until dissolved. Stir into the warmed wine mixture.

3 When the mixture has cooled to room temperature, add the cream and stir well. Pour the mixture into an oiled 5 cup (1.25 liter) mold. Chill for at least 3 hours (but not more than 48).

4 For the sauce, roughly mash the fruit, reserving a few whole pieces for decoration, then add the juice of 1 lime and the confectioners' sugar and mix well. Pass through a fine sieve.

5 Gently warm the mold to help loosen the gelatin by immersing it to the rim in warm water. Invert the gelatin onto a serving plate. Spoon the sauce around and decorate with whole fruits and mint leaves.

LIME & MINT
MOLD

89

SUMMER MENU FOR 6

BRIE & LENTIL SALAD

🥄 15 MINUTES 🍲 30 MINUTES

INGREDIENTS

1 TBSP VEGETABLE OIL

3 ONIONS, FINELY CHOPPED

2 GARLIC CLOVES, CRUSHED

1¼ CUPS (250G) LENTILS (PREFERABLY PUY)

1 LEMON, JUICE ONLY

2½ CUPS (600ML) WATER

4 SPRIGS FRESH THYME, PLUS 6 TO GARNISH

1 BAY LEAF

SALT & PEPPER TO TASTE

½ CUP (125ML) HAZELNUT DRESSING
(SEE PAGE 185)

¾ LB (375G) RIPE BRIE, THINLY SLICED

GREEN HERB LEAVES TO GARNISH

COOK'S TIP

Green or orange lentils need less time to cook; follow the package instructions if you use them.

1 Heat the oil in a saucepan, add the onions and garlic, and cook gently for about 5 minutes, until softened. Stir in the lentils, then pour on the lemon juice and water.

2 Add the thyme, bay leaf, and seasoning to the pan, bring to a boil, then simmer for approximately 20 minutes, until the lentils are *al dente* and the water has been absorbed.

Discard the thyme and bay leaf and drain the lentils thoroughly.

3 Return the lentils to the pan and stir in 4 tablespoons of Hazelnut Dressing. Let cool until the mixture reaches room temperature.

4 For each portion, fill a 2in (5cm) ring mold with the lentil mixture. Press down well and invert it carefully onto a plate. Arrange a few slices of Brie and green herb leaves on the same plate. Drizzle with the Hazelnut Dressing and season the Brie with freshly ground black pepper. Garnish each portion of lentils with a sprig of thyme.

BRIE & LENTIL
SALAD

TROUT WITH GOOSEBERRY SAUCE

25 MINUTES · 15 MINUTES

INGREDIENTS
½ LB (250G) GOOSEBERRIES
1½ TBSP SUGAR
4 TBSP WATER
¾ CUP (175G) BUTTER
½ TSP GROUND GINGER
6 TROUT (PREFERABLY RIVER OR BROWN),
FILLETED, CLEANED, FINS & GILLS
TRIMMED, HEADS LEFT ON
ALL-PURPOSE FLOUR TO DUST
SALT & PEPPER TO TASTE
4 TBSP OLIVE OIL
NEW POTATOES & SALAD GREENS TO SERVE
FLAT-LEAF PARSLEY TO GARNISH

1 To make the sauce, place the gooseberries, sugar, and water in a saucepan and simmer gently for 5 minutes, stirring occasionally until soft. Drain thoroughly.

2 Return the mix to the saucepan, beat in one-third of the butter, and the ginger to form a purée. Pour into a sauceboat and keep warm.

3 Dust the trout on each side with seasoned flour. In a large skillet, heat the olive oil with the remaining butter. Over moderate heat, cook each trout for about 4 minutes on each side, until golden.

4 Place 1 trout on each plate, pour over the gooseberry sauce, and garnish with flat-leaf parsley. Serve with new potatoes and a green salad.

COOK'S TIPS
If gooseberries are unavailable, use peeled, cored, roughly chopped cooking apples, with an extra tablespoon of water, or use ½ lb (250g) rhubarb. Cook the trout in 2 batches if necessary, keeping the prepared ones warm, covered, in the oven.

STRAWBERRY TART

20 MINUTES · 25 MINUTES

INGREDIENTS
SWEET SHORTCRUST PASTRY (SEE PAGE 184)
1¾ CUPS (400ML) HEAVY CREAM
1¾ CUPS (400ML) FROMAGE FRAIS
OR FARMER CHEESE
3 TBSP CONFECTIONERS' SUGAR SIFTED, PLUS
EXTRA TO DUST
1 TBSP ROSE WATER
1 PINT (500G) STRAWBERRIES (PREFERABLY
WILD)
4 TBSP RED CURRANT JELLY, MELTED

COOK'S TIPS
Raspberries can also be used instead of strawberries. The pastry case can be made two days in advance and kept in an airtight tin.

1 For the crust, roll out the pastry and press into a 10in (25cm) loose-bottomed fluted tart pan. Prick the bottom of the pastry all over with a fork, then refrigerate for 30 minutes to prevent it shrinking when baked.

2 Preheat oven to 350°F/180°C. Line the dough with waxed paper, fill with dried beans, and bake for 15 minutes, until the pastry is just set. Remove the beans and waxed paper. Return to the oven for 15 minutes longer, until the pastry is crisp and golden. Let cool.

3 To make the filling, beat the cream, fromage frais, confectioners' sugar, and rose water until thick and spread over the pastry base. Arrange the strawberries on top in the pastry shell.

4 Brush the strawberries with the cooled red currant jelly to glaze. Dust the edge of the pastry shell with confectioners' sugar and serve.

VEGETARIAN FOR 6

ROAST TOMATO SOUP

🥄 15 MINUTES 🍲 1 HOUR 35 MINUTES

INGREDIENTS
4LB (2KG) FRESH PLUM TOMATOES
5 TBSP (75ML) OLIVE OIL
1 TBSP EACH FENNEL & CUMIN SEED
2 COARSELY CHOPPED ONIONS
2 FRESH GREEN CHILIES, SEEDED
& FINELY CHOPPED
4 GARLIC CLOVES, COARSELY CHOPPED
4 KAFFIR LIME LEAVES
2 LIMES, JUICE & GRATED ZEST
1 TBSP SOFT BROWN SUGAR
2½ CUPS (600ML) WATER
2 TBSP TOMATO PASTE
5 TBSP COARSELY CHOPPED FRESH BASIL
SALT & PEPPER TO TASTE
SOUR CREAM TO SERVE

1 Preheat oven to 400°F/200°C. Slice the tomatoes in half, brush with 3 tablespoons of the olive oil, and place cut face up on a lined baking sheet. Roast for 1 hour.

2 Meanwhile, in a heavy skillet, dry roast the fennel and cumin for about 3 minutes, until fragrant. Let them cool, then grind using a mortar and pestle or an electric grinder.

3 Heat the remaining oil. Gently fry the onions, chilies, and garlic for about 8 minutes, until they are softened and just beginning to brown.

4 When the tomatoes are roasted, combine all the ingredients, except the basil and sour cream, in a large saucepan. Bring to a boil and simmer gently for 20 minutes.

5 Discard the kaffir lime leaves. Adjust the seasoning to taste. Process the soup in a blender with the fresh basil until smooth. Serve with a swirl of sour cream.

COOK'S TIPS
Use other tomatoes if plum are not available. If you cannot find kaffir lime leaves (Oriental stores stock them), use the grated zest of 2 limes.

BLUE CHEESE SOUFFLÉS

🥄 15 MINUTES 🍲 20 MINUTES

INGREDIENTS
¼ LB (100G) STILTON (OR OTHER HARD
BLUE-VEINED CHEESE)
4 TBSP FRESH BASIL, COARSELY CHOPPED
7 TBSP (105G) BUTTER
½ CUP (75G) ALL-PURPOSE FLOUR, SIFTED
SALT TO TASTE
2 CUPS (500ML) MILK
6 LARGE EGGS, SEPARATED: 6 WHITES, 4 YOLKS

COOK'S TIPS
This recipe is not suitable for more than 6, because the soufflés must be eaten immediately. Placing the baking sheet in the preheating oven to warm helps the soufflés to rise.

1 Preheat oven to 350°F/180°C. Place the Stilton and basil in a food processor and work until it is the consistency of coarse bread crumbs.

2 Heat the butter in a saucepan. Mix together the flour, salt, and milk, and gradually add to the butter, stirring constantly. Cook over very low heat for 5 minutes, stirring constantly, until thickened and smooth. Remove from the heat and stir in the cheese mixture. Let cool slightly.

3 Whisk the egg whites with a pinch of salt until they form stiff peaks.

4 Place the cheese sauce into a large mixing bowl. Add the 4 egg yolks and beat lightly until well mixed. Carefully fold in a quarter of the egg whites, then add the remainder until just combined.

5 Spoon the mixture into 12 greased 3in (7cm) ramekins or soufflé dishes until full. Place on a warmed baking sheet and bake for about 15 minutes, or until the tops are just set. Serve immediately with steamed chard and asparagus.

COFFEE TRUFFLE PUDDINGS

⏱ 15 MINUTES 🍲 20 MINUTES

INGREDIENTS

½ CUP (125G) UNSALTED BUTTER, SOFTENED
½ CUP & 1 TBSP (150G) SUGAR
4 TSP INSTANT COFFEE GRANULES,
DISSOLVED IN 1 TBSP HOT WATER
2 LARGE EGGS
½ CUP (125G) ALL-PURPOSE FLOUR, SIFTED
1 TSP BAKING POWDER, SIFTED
6 DARK CHOCOLATE TRUFFLES
½ CUP (125G) LIGHT CREAM
1 TSP VANILLA EXTRACT

COOK'S TIP

Rum truffles are particularly good, as is a teaspoon of rum added to the cream sauce.

1 Preheat oven to 375°F/190°C. Cream the butter, ½ cup (125g) of the sugar, and coffee until fluffy. Gradually add the eggs until they are well combined. Do not overbeat. Fold in the flour and baking powder.

2 Grease 6 x 2½ in (6cm) ramekins. Place 1 heaped tablespoon of mixture into each ramekin, then set a truffle on top. Spoon over more mixture, ensuring that it completely surrounds the truffle, until the ramekins are three-quarters full.

Bake for 15–18 minutes, until the puddings are springy to the touch.

3 Meanwhile, make the sauce. Gently heat the cream, remaining sugar, and vanilla in a saucepan. Stir until the sugar has dissolved.

4 Remove the ramekins from the oven and let stand for 5 minutes before unmolding onto individual plates. Serve warm, surrounded by the creamy sauce.

BLUE CHEESE
SOUFFLÉS

FRUITS OF THE SEA FOR 6

SHRIMP IN HARD CIDER

— 🥄 25 MINUTES 🍲 8 MINUTES —

INGREDIENTS

30 LARGE SHRIMP, ABOUT 1LB (500G)
2 TBSP SUNFLOWER OIL
2 GARLIC CLOVES, SKINS LEFT ON, CRUSHED
UNDER THE FLAT OF A KNIFE
4 TBSP CALVADOS OR BRANDY
1 CUP (250ML) STRONG DRY HARD CIDER
BREAD & BUTTER TO SERVE
SALAD GREENS TO GARNISH

1 To prepare the shrimp, break or cut off the head and peel off the shell, leaving the tail on. With a small, sharp knife, make a shallow cut along the center back; remove the dark intestinal vein. Pat dry with paper towels.

2 Heat the oil in a skillet until very hot, then add the garlic and the shrimp, and cook for about 1 minute on each side, until they turn pink. Transfer to a warmed dish to keep hot in the oven.

3 Add the Calvados to the pan and carefully set fire to it. When the flames have died, add the cider. Boil until the liquid has almost gone.

4 Discard the garlic. Return the shrimp to the pan, stirring, to coat them in the sauce. Serve with bread and butter and salad leaves to garnish.

COOK'S TIP
Drink hard cider as an excellent accompaniment to this delicious northern French appetizer.

TUNA STEAKS WITH RHUBARB

— 🥄 20 MINUTES 🍲 15 MINUTES —

INGREDIENTS

2LB (1KG) TUNA STEAK
SALT & PEPPER TO TASTE
6 TBSP (90ML) OLIVE OIL
1¼ CUPS (300ML) PORT OR MEDIUM DRY
SHERRY
3 TBSP BALSAMIC VINEGAR
½ LB (250G) RHUBARB, STALKS ONLY, CUT
INTO ½ IN (1CM) PIECES
1 TBSP FISH SAUCE
1¼ CUPS (300ML) VEGETABLE STOCK
(SEE PAGE 185)
SUGAR TO TASTE
½ ORANGE, JUICE & GRATED ZEST
SALAD GREENS & HERB LEAVES TO SERVE

1 Rub the seasoning into the tuna. Heat 1 tablespoon of oil in a large skillet over high heat. When the oil is hot, sear the tuna all over.

2 Turn the heat to medium and cook for 6 minutes longer, turning occasionally. Transfer to a warmed dish, covered, to keep hot in the oven.

3 To make the sauce, pour the port and 2 tablespoons of the vinegar into the pan, scraping any remaining browned bits of tuna, and stir. Cook over moderate heat until the liquid is reduced by half. Add the rhubarb, fish sauce, and stock and again reduce by half. Taste and add a pinch of sugar if necessary.

4 To make the dressing, combine the remaining vinegar, the remaining oil, the orange juice and zest. Mix well, and season if necessary.

5 Cut the tuna into slices, approximately ¼ in (5mm) thick (the fish should be very rare). To serve, put a few mixed salad and herb leaves on each plate and spoon over the orange dressing. Arrange the tuna slices on the same plate and pour over the rhubarb sauce.

COOK'S TIP
Tuna is best served rare, but you should check with your guests first in case anyone would prefer a slightly more cooked steak.

TUNA STEAKS
WITH
RHUBARB

MANGO SYLLABUB & ALMOND COOKIES

—— ⏱ 40 MINUTES 🍲 6 MINUTES ——

INGREDIENTS

3 RIPE MANGOES, PEELED, STONE REMOVED
& COARSELY CHOPPED

3 TBSP SUPERFINE SUGAR

1 LIME, JUICE & GRATED ZEST

⅔ CUP (150ML) MANGO JUICE

4 TBSP KIRSCH

2 CUPS (450ML) HEAVY CREAM

¾ CUP (90G) ALL-PURPOSE FLOUR, SIFTED

¾ CUP (175G) CONFECTIONERS' SUGAR, SIFTED

1 CUP (175G) SLICED ALMONDS

⅓ CUP (90ML) ORANGE JUICE

2 DROPS ALMOND EXTRACT

½ CUP (125G) UNSALTED BUTTER, MELTED

1 To make the syllabub, add the mango to the superfine sugar, lime juice and zest, mango juice, and Kirsch. Blend in a food processor until smooth.

2 Whisk the cream until it just begins to thicken, then beat in the mango mixture until the cream holds its shape. Spoon into wine glasses or individual dishes and chill until needed.

3 To make the cookies, preheat oven to 400°F/200°C. Mix the flour, confectioners' sugar, and almonds in a large bowl. Add the orange juice, almond extract, and butter. Mix well.

4 Line a baking sheet with baking parchment and place about 30 heaped teaspoons of the mixture roughly 4in (10cm) apart. Smooth down the mixture to make rounds.

5 Bake for 6 minutes, or until golden. Leave on the baking sheet for 1 minute, then transfer to a wire rack to cool. Serve the almond cookies with the mango syllabub.

COOK'S TIP

For curved cookies, wrap them around a rolling pin to shape while they are still hot.

HARVEST SUPPER FOR 6

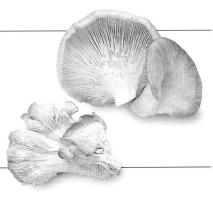

WILD MUSHROOM RAGOÛT

⏱ 15 MINUTES 🍲 15 MINUTES

INGREDIENTS

2 LB (1 KG) WILD MUSHROOMS
SALT TO TASTE
2 TBSP OLIVE OIL
2 GARLIC CLOVES, SKINS LEFT ON, CRUSHED
UNDER THE FLAT OF A KNIFE
1 CUP (250 ML) SWEET VERMOUTH, MEDIUM
DRY SHERRY, OR SWEET WHITE WINE
1 TBSP GROUND CORIANDER
½ TSP GROUND NUTMEG
2 FRESH TARRAGON SPRIGS
FRESH CILANTRO, FINELY CHOPPED,
TO GARNISH

1 To prepare the mushrooms, scrape away the dirt with a sharp knife and wipe clean with paper towels. Never let wild mushrooms soak in water. Cut the mushrooms into bite-sized pieces, discarding the stalks, and sprinkle with salt.

2 Heat the oil in a large skillet, and gently cook the mushrooms with the garlic over high heat for about 8 minutes, stirring constantly, until the mushrooms are almost cooked.

3 Add the vermouth, ground coriander, nutmeg, and tarragon, and cook rapidly for approximately 5 minutes, until the vermouth has reduced to about 6 tablespoons (90ml). Discard the garlic and tarragon sprigs. Garnish with fresh cilantro and serve with garlic bread or lightly toasted brioche sprinkled with sea salt.

COOK'S TIP

Wild mushrooms can be difficult and expensive to obtain; this dish will also be delicious with a combination of cultivated varieties such as field, button, horse, and chestnut mushrooms.

WILD
MUSHROOM
RAGOÛT

PHEASANT & APPLES WITH CALVADOS
☑ 20 MINUTES 🍲 20 MINUTES

INGREDIENTS
4 TART APPLES (PREFERABLY GRANNY SMITHS)
1 LEMON, JUICE ONLY
4 TBSP BUTTER
4 TBSP OLIVE OIL
6 PHEASANT BREASTS, BONED & SKINNED
2 TSP SUGAR
SALT & PEPPER TO TASTE
4 TBSP CALVADOS OR BRANDY
1 CUP (250ML) DRY WHITE WINE
4 TBSP CRÈME FRAÎCHE OR SOUR CREAM
SPINACH & HERBY POTATOES
(SEE PAGE 186) TO SERVE

1 Cut the apples into quarters and remove the cores, then cut each quarter into 4 slices. Shake them in a bowl with half of the lemon juice.

2 In a large skillet, heat half each of the butter and olive oil, and gently cook the apples for 3 minutes, until golden. Transfer to a warmed ovenproof dish to keep hot.

3 In the same pan, heat the rest of the butter and olive oil. Add the pheasant, sprinkle with the sugar and the remaining lemon juice, season, and cook until pale golden on both sides. Turn heat to low, cover, and cook for 4–5 minutes on each side. Transfer to the ovenproof dish to keep hot.

4 To make the sauce, turn heat to medium and heat the Calvados in the same pan. Scrape the browned bits around the sides and stir. Almost immediately set light to the alcohol.

5 When the flames have died, add the wine, and bring to a boil, then simmer until reduced by half. Whisk in the crème fraîche and stir until smooth. Arrange the pheasant on a bed of cooked spinach and surround with the apples and Herby Potatoes. Pour over the sauce.

COOK'S TIP
Chicken or guinea fowl breasts make a delicious alternative to pheasant.

CHOCOLATE & COFFEE CHEESECAKE
☑ 30 MINUTES 🍲 35 MINUTES 🍶 8 HOURS CHILLING

INGREDIENTS
7 TBSP (100G) UNSALTED BUTTER, MELTED
8OZ (250G) AMARETTI COOKIES,
CRUSHED TO FINE CRUMBS
2/3 CUP (125G) SLIVERED ALMONDS,
TOASTED & FINELY CHOPPED
1½ LB (750G) CREAM CHEESE, SOFTENED
¾ CUP (175G) SUGAR
3 LARGE EGGS, LIGHTLY BEATEN
3 LEMONS, GRATED ZEST
2 TSP VANILLA EXTRACT
3 TBSP INSTANT COFFEE GRANULES,
DISSOLVED IN 1 TBSP HOT WATER
5OZ (150G) PLAIN DARK CHOCOLATE, MELTED
½ CUP (125ML) HEAVY CREAM, WARMED
LIGHT CREAM & COFFEE LIQUEUR TO SERVE

1 To make the crust, mix the butter with the amaretti and almonds in a food processor. Turn the mixture into a 9in (23cm) lined and greased spring-form cake pan, pressing it around the base and sides with the back of a spoon.

2 Preheat oven to 350°F/180°C. For the filling, beat the cream cheese with the sugar until just smooth. Add the eggs, lemon zest, and vanilla and beat until just blended. Divide the mixture into 2 bowls. Into one of the bowls, stir in the coffee. Into the other, stir the melted chocolate and cream.

3 Cover the crust with a large spoonful of the coffee mixture, followed by a large spoonful of the chocolate and cream mixture. Repeat until both are used up. With the end of a spoon, swirl the mixture around to create a marbled effect.

4 Place the cake in the middle of the oven and bake for 30 minutes. Let cool, then refrigerate for 8 hours or more in the pan. Release the sides of the pan, and serve with light cream flavored with coffee liqueur.

COOK'S TIPS
The cake will not appear cooked when it is first removed from the oven, but will set as it chills. It is very rich and could serve 10–12 in small slices.

WINTER DINNER FOR 6

SHRIMP, LEEK & SAFFRON SOUP

15 MINUTES   30 MINUTES

INGREDIENTS
24 LARGE SHRIMP, ABOUT 1 LB (500G)
⅔ CUP (150G) BUTTER
6 LEEKS, COARSELY CHOPPED
4 TBSP BRANDY
2 CUPS (500ML) DRY VERMOUTH
OR DRY WHITE WINE
2 CUPS (500ML) FISH STOCK (SEE PAGE 185)
1 BAY LEAF
3 TBSP FRESH DILL, FINELY CHOPPED, PLUS
SPRIGS TO GARNISH
1 TSP SAFFRON THREADS, CRUSHED
SALT & PEPPER TO TASTE
SCANT 1 CUP (200ML) HEAVY CREAM

1 Prepare the shrimps (see Step 1, page 94). Heat the butter in a medium-size saucepan, add the leeks, and cook gently for about 7 minutes, until softened. Add the brandy. After 10 seconds, carefully set it alight, then allow the flame to go out.

2 Add the vermouth, fish stock, bay leaf, chopped dill, and saffron, bring to a boil, and simmer for 20 minutes. Remove the bay leaf; season. Blend the soup in a food processor until smooth, and return to the pan.

3 Add the shrimps and cook for 2 minutes, until they turn pink. Stir in the cream and heat through until almost boiling. Serve in warmed soup bowls, garnished with sprigs of dill.

COOK'S TIP
One teaspoon of loosely packed saffron threads is equal to a quarter teaspoon of ground saffron.

FLEMISH-STYLE BEEF

25 MINUTES   3¼ HOURS

INGREDIENTS
3½ LB (1.75KG) PIECE OF SIRLOIN BEEF
SALT TO TASTE
1 TBSP VEGETABLE OIL
4 ONIONS, COARSELY CHOPPED
4 GARLIC CLOVES, FINELY CHOPPED
4 CARROTS, CUT INTO THICK SLICES
4 CLOVES, CRUSHED
½ ORANGE, ZEST ONLY (IN STRIPS)
4 TBSP BRANDY
5 CUPS (1.25 LITERS) DARK BEER
1 TBSP PEPPERCORNS, CRUSHED
2 BAY LEAVES
4 SPRIGS FRESH THYME
2 TBSP DRIED PORCINI, GROUND (OPTIONAL)
4 TBSP RED WINE VINEGAR
2 TBSP CORNSTARCH
2 TBSP LIGHT BROWN SUGAR
BRAISED FENNEL & NEW POTATOES TO SERVE

1 Preheat oven to 325°F/160°C. Season the beef with salt. Heat the oil in a large skillet and brown on all sides for approximately 5 minutes. Transfer to a casserole just large enough for the beef and vegetables. Return the skillet to the heat.

2 Gently cook the onions, garlic, carrots, cloves, and orange zest for 5 minutes, and spoon them into the casserole, surrounding the meat.

3 Place the casserole over medium heat. Pour in the brandy and carefully set it alight. When the flames have died, add the beer, peppercorns, bay leaves, thyme, and ground porcini, if using. Bring to a boil.

4 Place a sheet of foil over the casserole, then cover it with the lid. Cook in the oven for 3 hours. When done, transfer the beef and vegetables to a carving plate and keep warm. Reserve the juices in the casserole.

5 To make the sauce, mix the vinegar, cornstarch, and sugar in a bowl until smooth. Add 2 tablespoons of meat juices and mix well. Pour into the casserole and cook over low heat for 10 minutes, stirring constantly. Carve and serve the beef and vegetables with braised fennel and new potatoes.

COOK'S TIP
Cook this dish a day or two ahead for an even better flavor. Reheat in a moderate oven.

FLEMISH-STYLE
BEEF

STEAMED CRANBERRY PUDDING

30 MINUTES · 1 HOUR 35 MINUTES

INGREDIENTS
¾ CUP (175G) BUTTER
1 CUP (200G) SUGAR
1½ CUPS (175G) SELF-RISING FLOUR, SIFTED
1 TSP BAKING POWDER, SIFTED
3 LARGE EGGS, LIGHTLY BEATEN
2 LIMES, JUICE & GRATED ZEST
3 CUPS (300G) CRANBERRIES
4 TBSP MARMALADE
1 CUP (250ML) ORANGE JUICE
2 TBSP CONFECTIONERS' SUGAR, SIFTED
2 TSP ANGOSTURA BITTERS

1 Cream the butter and ¾ cup (175g) of the sugar until pale and fluffy. Add the flour, baking powder, eggs, half of the lime juice and zest, and 1 cup (125g) of the cranberries, coarsely chopped. Mix well.

2 Grease an 8 cup (2 liter) pudding mold, then sprinkle the remaining sugar over the interior. Cover the bottom with ½ cup (60g) cranberries, spoon over the marmalade, then add the cake mixture.

3 Cover the top of the mold with lightly greased waxed paper, then cover this with a large sheet of foil that has been pleated once to allow the pudding to expand. Tie tightly in position with string. Steam over gently simmering water in a large lidded pot for 1½ hours.

4 To make the sauce, blend the remaining cranberries and lime juice and zest with the orange juice, confectioners' sugar, and bitters. Heat and serve with the pudding.

COOK'S TIP
You can use a soufflé dish instead of a pudding mold to cook this dessert.

FAMILY GATHERING FOR 12

ITALIAN CABBAGE SOUP

15 MINUTES   17 MINUTES

INGREDIENTS
1 TBSP VEGETABLE OIL
10OZ (300G) SMOKED PANCETTA
OR BACON, SLICED
1 SAVOY CABBAGE, COARSELY CHOPPED
8 CUPS (2 LITERS) CHICKEN STOCK (SEE
PAGE 185)
SALT & PEPPER TO TASTE
1LB (500G) GRUYÈRE CHEESE, CUBED
½LB (250G) WHITE BREAD, CRUSTS REMOVED,
CUT INTO ¾ IN (2CM) CUBES
10 SPRIGS EACH FRESH THYME & MARJORAM
2 BAY LEAVES
¾ CUP (200G) BUTTER, IN PIECES

1 Heat the oil in a skillet, add the pancetta, and sauté over moderate heat for 10 minutes, until crisp. Drain on paper towels.

2 Cook the cabbage in a large saucepan of salted boiling water for 2 minutes. Refresh under cold water and drain.

3 Heat the stock until it comes to a boil. Adjust seasoning to taste.

4 In a large saucepan, place in layers one-third of the cabbage, followed by one-third each of the Gruyère, bread, pancetta, and herbs. Repeat these layers twice more.

5 Pour over the boiling stock and bring back to a boil over high heat. Add the butter pieces and simmer for 5 minutes. Discard the bay leaves and thyme stalks and serve immediately, without stirring the soup.

COOK'S TIPS
Serve the soup using a mug with a handle to dip deep into the pan. Halve the recipe to make a homey winter supper dish for 6 people.

SPICY PORK ROAST

25 MINUTES   2 HOURS   24 HOURS MARINATING

INGREDIENTS
¾ CUP (175ML) SUNFLOWER OIL
⅔ CUP (150ML) DARK RUM
⅔ CUP (150ML) LIGHT SOY SAUCE
⅔ CUP (150ML) HONEY
2 LIMES, JUICE & GRATED ZEST
6 GARLIC CLOVES, CRUSHED
2 TBSP GROUND BLACK PEPPER
2 TBSP PAPRIKA
1 TBSP FENNEL SEED, CRUSHED
2 TSP GROUND GINGER
4LB (2KG) LOIN OF PORK
24 SHALLOTS, ABOUT ¾LB (400G), PEELED
1½LB (750G) CARROTS, CUT INTO CHUNKS
10 FRESH THYME SPRIGS
4 BAY LEAVES
BAY ROAST POTATOES (SEE PAGE 187) TO SERVE

1 To make the marinade, place ⅔ cup (150ml) of the oil, rum, soy sauce, honey, lime juice and zest, garlic, pepper, paprika, fennel, and ginger in a large nonmetallic bowl. Mix well.

2 Pierce the pork all over with a sharp fork and rub the marinade into the meat. Cover and marinate in the refrigerator for 24 hours, turning occasionally.

3 Preheat oven to 325°F/160°C. Remove the pork and reserve the marinade. Heat the remaining oil in a skillet and, when it is fairly hot, brown the pork on all sides.

4 In a large casserole, place the pork and the marinade. Surround the pork with the shallots, carrots, and the herbs. Cover with a sheet of foil and the casserole lid.

5 Cook the pork in the oven for 2 hours. Baste and turn the meat approximately every 30 minutes. Carve the meat into slices ¼ in (5mm) thick and serve with the carrots and shallots, and Bay Roast Potatoes.

COOK'S TIP
If the liquid almost disappears in roasting, add 2 to 3 tablespoons of water.

MIRACULOUS BLACKBERRY CAKE

1 HOUR 45 MINUTES　　1 HOUR 25 MINUTES

INGREDIENTS

7 EGGS: 3 WHITES ONLY, 4 WHOLE
PINCH OF CREAM OF TARTAR
1 CUP (175G) DARK BROWN SUGAR, SIFTED
½ LB (250G) BUTTER, SOFTENED
1 CUP (250G) SUPERFINE SUGAR
2 CUPS (250G) SELF-RISING FLOUR, SIFTED
2 TSP BAKING POWDER, SIFTED
2 TSP VANILLA EXTRACT
2 CUPS (450ML) HEAVY CREAM
2 TBSP CRÈME DE MÛRE (OPTIONAL)
3 TBSP BLACKBERRY JAM
1½ CUPS (175G) BLACKBERRIES

1 To make the meringue, preheat oven to 275°F/140°C. Whisk the egg whites with cream of tartar until they form soft peaks. Gradually add the dark brown sugar, whisking after each addition, until the peaks hold firm.

2 With a pencil, draw 2 x 7½ in (19cm) circles on waxed paper and place each on a baking sheet. Using a plain ½ in (1cm) nozzle, pipe the meringue mixture, starting at the circle centers and spiraling outward as far as the pencil lines. Bake for 1 hour. Set the meringues aside to cool.

3 Preheat oven to 350°F/180°C. For the cake, beat the butter, superfine sugar, flour, baking powder, eggs, and vanilla. Spoon the mixture into 2 lined and greased 8in (20cm) springform cake pans. Bake for 30 minutes. Leave the cakes in their pans for 10 minutes, then transfer to a wire rack.

4 Whisk together the cream and Crème de Mûre, if using, until stiff peaks have formed. Spread jam over the surface of each cake layer.

5 Place one layer on a serving plate and spread one-fifth of the cream over the jam. Lay one meringue on top and, again, spread with one-fifth of the cream. Add the second layer and repeat the layers, finishing with the cream. Top with blackberries and cream piping made from the rest of the cream.

COOK'S TIPS

The meringue and sponges can be made a day in advance and stored in airtight containers. However, it is best to assemble the cake at the last moment, because the cream and berries will soften the meringue.

MIRACULOUS
BLACKBERRY CAKE

COUNTRY FOOD FOR 6

ASPARAGUS & HAM FETTUCCINE

☑ 10 MINUTES 🍲 15 MINUTES

INGREDIENTS
¾ LB (375G) ASPARAGUS
2 TBSP OLIVE OIL
¼ LB (125G) SMOKED HAM, SLICED
2 GARLIC CLOVES, SKINS LEFT ON, CRUSHED
UNDER THE FLAT OF A KNIFE
¼ LB (125G) FROZEN PEAS, THAWED
1¼ LB (625G) FETTUCCINE
SCANT 1 CUP (200ML) HEAVY CREAM
½ TSP GRATED NUTMEG
1 CUP (100G) GRATED PARMESAN CHEESE,
PLUS EXTRA FOR TOPPING
SALT & PEPPER TO TASTE

1 Snap any woody ends off the asparagus spears. Cook in a saucepan of salted boiling water for 6 minutes, or until *al dente*. Drain.

2 Heat the olive oil in a skillet. Add the ham and garlic and cook for 3 minutes, until the ham just begins to brown, then add the peas and asparagus. Cook for another 2 minutes.

3 Cook the fettuccine in a large saucepan with plenty of salted boiling water for 6 minutes if dried, 5–6 minutes if fresh, until *al dente*.

4 Drain the pasta, then return it to the pan. Add the cream and heat through, stirring constantly, until it begins to thicken. Stir in the asparagus and ham mixture, nutmeg, Parmesan, and seasoning. Serve immediately, with a little Parmesan sprinkled over the top of each portion.

VEGETABLE & NUT KEBABS

☑ 35 MINUTES 🍲 65 MINUTES

INGREDIENTS
½ LB (250G) SMALL POTATOES, SCRUBBED
½ LB (250G) OF EACH OF THE FOLLOWING, CUT
INTO CHUNKS: PUMPKIN (SEEDED), ACORN
SQUASH (SEEDED), CELERIAC, TURNIPS, PARSNIPS
⅔ CUP (150ML) OLIVE OIL
5 TBSP (75G) ALL-PURPOSE FLOUR
SALT & PEPPER TO TASTE
1½ CUPS (250G) BRAZIL NUTS
3 TBSP WATER
3 SHALLOTS, COARSELY CHOPPED
3 GARLIC CLOVES, COARSELY CHOPPED
1IN (2.5CM) PIECE OF FRESH GINGER,
PEELED & COARSELY CHOPPED
1 CUP (90G) ROASTED PEANUTS (UNSALTED)
1 TBSP FENNEL SEED
2 CUPS (500ML) COCONUT MILK
SALAD GREENS & WALNUT DRESSING
(SEE PAGE 185) TO SERVE

1 Bring a large saucepan of salted water to a boil, add all the vegetables, bring back to a boil, then drain immediately.

2 Preheat oven to 425°F/220°C. As soon as the vegetables are cool enough to handle, toss them in 2 tablespoons of oil, then roll in flour. Thread alternately onto long skewers, allowing 3 per person.

3 Coat the bases of 2 baking sheets with olive oil, about 3 tablespoons per sheet, and heat in the oven. When the oil is hot, lay the kebabs on the sheets. Bake for 45 minutes, turning the kebabs once. Add the Brazil nuts 20 minutes before the end of cooking.

4 Meanwhile, make the sauce. In a food processor, blend the water with the shallots, garlic, ginger, peanuts, fennel seed, and salt.

5 Heat the remaining oil in a skillet and add the processed sauce ingredients. Cook gently for 5 minutes, then stir in the coconut milk. Cook uncovered over low heat for 10 minutes. Serve the kebabs and Brazil nuts with the sauce and a green salad with Walnut Dressing.

COOK'S TIP
If the vegetables appear to be browning too much during cooking, cover loosely with foil.

SPICED QUINCES
& EARL GREY
SORBET

SPICED QUINCES & EARL GREY SORBET

10 MINUTES — 40 MINUTES — 12 HOURS CHILLING

INGREDIENTS
2 LARGE QUINCES
3 CUPS (750ML) SWEET WHITE WINE
2 LEMONS, JUICE & GRATED ZEST
2 FRESH ROSEMARY SPRIGS
4 TBSP HONEY (PREFERABLY ACACIA)
3 EARL GREY TEA BAGS
1½ CUPS (375G) WATER
1½ CUPS (375G) SUGAR
2 LIMES, JUICE & GRATED ZEST,
RESERVING ZEST TO DECORATE
1 LARGE EGG, WHITE ONLY

COOK'S TIPS
If quinces are unavailable, use pears (preferably Comice variety) instead. If using an ice-cream maker, follow the manufacturer's instructions.

1 To make the spiced quinces, cut the fruit into quarters, remove the cores, then cut each quarter into 3 wedge-shaped slices.

2 In a saucepan, heat half of the wine (chill the rest for the sorbet). Add the quinces, lemon juice and zest, rosemary, honey, and 1 tea bag.

3 Poach the quinces for 15–20 minutes, until they are just cooked. Discard the tea bag and transfer the quince slices to a serving dish.

4 Return the pan to the heat and reduce the liquid to about 6 tablespoons (90ml). Pour it over the quinces and refrigerate overnight.

5 To make the sorbet, heat the water in a saucepan with the sugar and 2 tea bags. Bring almost to a boil, stirring until the sugar has dissolved to make a syrup. Discard the tea bags. Let syrup cool, then refrigerate for at least 2 hours, until completely chilled.

6 Pour the syrup, juice and zest of 2 limes, and the remaining wine into a rigid freezerproof container. Cover and freeze for 3 hours, stirring at the end of each hour. On the final stirring, lightly beat the egg white and stir into the sorbet. Refreeze for at least 3 hours. Transfer to the refrigerator 30 minutes before serving to soften. Decorate with lime zest and serve with the quinces.

BUFFET PARTIES

WINING AND DINING MORE THAN TWELVE GUESTS IS MOST EASILY EXECUTED WITH A BUFFET. THERE ARE PLENTY OF EASY DISHES YOU CAN PREPARE WELL IN ADVANCE OR, IF YOU PREFER TO LIVE DANGEROUSLY, AFTER YOUR GUESTS HAVE ARRIVED! PLAN AND ADHERE TO A METICULOUS WORK SCHEDULE, COOK FLAVORFUL FOOD THAT IS SIMPLE TO EAT, AND A RELAXED AND SOCIABLE CELEBRATION WILL BE ASSURED.

The Champagne Buffet menu (page 113), with its Marinated Salmon, Chicken Crepe Stack, and Savarin, is especially appropriate for Christmas celebrations (right).

CHRISTMAS

Pile the tables with delectable treats – it is

FOLLOW OR ADAPT the many decorative traditions the festive season has to offer to make your Christmas party memorable.

PERSONAL GIFTS
A gift that is stylishly wrapped in customized paper becomes even more of a treat for the recipient.

WRAPPING PAPER

Make simple gift wrap using tissue paper and spray paints. Follow the steps below, or create a random effect by crumpling up the paper before you spray.

1 For paper with a bold square pattern, pleat a sheet of colored tissue paper to make ¾–2in (2–5cm) folds. The pattern varies according to the width of the folds.

2 Place the paper in a cardboard box or on newspaper in a well-ventilated area. Release the folds (but don't smooth flat) and spray paint across the front of each one.

3 Allow the paint to dry, then pleat the paper again at right angles to the first folds. Repeat step 2, using a different-colored paint if you wish.

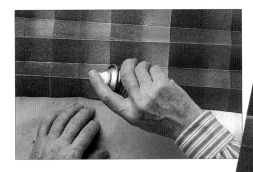

time to celebrate

MAROON BREAD BASKET
Line a bread basket with a pretty coordinated napkin to make a country loaf cut into wedges as much a decoration as a part of the meal.

LAYOUT OF THE TABLE
The buffet table, placed against a wall, is arranged with the items needed for each course grouped together. Any decorative elements are out of the way, at the back.

FRUIT ARRANGEMENT
A terra-cotta bowl brimming with fruit, a few candles, and a few simple flowers is an impressive decoration for a festive buffet table.

A CHRISTMAS TREE FOR THE WALL

Hang this long-lasting Christmas tree, decorated with fruit and glittering lights, on the wall like a picture, where it will not take up much space. The frame and its chicken-wire covering are easy to assemble and can be kept to reuse from year to year, replacing the moss and foliage. Suspend nuts, chocolates, and store-bought decorations on the tree, too.

1 ◁ Make a triangular frame from three pieces of bamboo, two the same length and one slightly shorter, wired together with florists' wires. Cover the frame with a double layer of chicken wire.

2 ▷ Twist the open ends of the chicken wire together to secure it around the frame, leaving a gap through which to fill with sphagnum moss. Pack the frame with moss, then close the gap.

Moss must be firm, but not too compacted

3 ▷ Poke sprigs of conifer – here fir because it does not drop its needles – into the moss-filled frame. Start at the bottom with larger pieces, overlapping to cover as you work up.

4 ▷ Thread a wire through each fruit, hooking one end and pulling it back gently into the fruit. Poke the free wire end through the frame from the front; bend at the back to secure.

5 ▷ Make holes for the fairy lights with a pencil. Starting at the top with the nonplug end, push each bulb through from the back, keeping the cord at the back and finishing with the plug near the tree's base.

Attach a hanging hook at top

Wire on a piece of bark for the trunk

108

Lime

DECORATIONS
The tree is hung with limes, tree tomatoes, and eggplant, which can be replaced if they look tired.

CHRISTMAS CONIFERS
Although conifers such as the fir here are usually associated with Christmas, other evergreens – laurel and skimmia, perhaps – would make an attractive change.

Tree tomato

White eggplant

ALFRESCO

"The greatest dishes are very simple dishes."

WHEN THE WEATHER IS FAIR, serve an appetizing and relaxed buffet lunch outdoors in your garden. Set it up out of the sun but near the house, so that hot food does not cool too much on its way to the table.

ICE BOWL

Very beautiful, yet simple to make, ice bowls last for over an hour in the shade, once out of the freezer. Choose plants that are in season.

Alstroemeria · Sweet pea · Eustoma · St. John's wort

BUFFET TABLE
The table is informally laid for guests to help themselves to all courses. Wine and glasses are to one side, away from the food, for easy replenishment.

1 Place one bowl inside another 1¼–1¾ in (3–4cm) larger in diameter. Half fill the outer bowl with water, adding a little milk or food coloring for a frosted effect.

2 Gently fill the inner bowl with water so that it sinks to the same level as the outer bowl. Hold it straight in a central position, and secure with adhesive tape.

3 Wedge nontoxic plant material into the water. Freeze for at least 8 hours. To release, pour cold water into the inner bowl, and partially submerge the outer bowl in cold, never warm, water. After a minute, ease the ice bowl free.

GEORGE AUGUSTE ESCOFFIER 1846–1935

CHILI POT
Fill little terra-cotta pots with chilies emerging from a ruff of foliage, their ends fanned out like a fountain. Being small, these pots do not clutter the table.

FROSTED SERVING BOWL
An ice bowl is a fitting and attractive receptacle from which to serve sorbet and ice cream. Fill with scoops of softened ice cream just before serving.

MENUS

The tables groan with food and the guests

BIRTHDAY PARTY

❧

Hearty cassoulet is a meal all by itself, but you'll want to team it with the lightest of chocolate birthday cakes for a special celebration. *Serves 18*

CASSOULET
Tasty beans and tender meats are all perfumed with herbs to make this unusual dish from southwest France.

CHOCOLATE BIRTHDAY CAKE
This beautifully decorated flourless cake is both rich and very light.

DRINKS
Partner the cassoulet with a good dry Graves, which comes from the same part of France. A demi-sec Champagne, served with the birthday cake, is both delicious and good for toasting.

PLANNING NOTES
The cassoulet improves with time; keep it covered in the refrigerator for a couple of days. Heat it in a moderate oven when ready to eat. If the cassoulet seems dry, add enough white wine during cooking to make the mixture just moist. The cake and its chocolate covering are best eaten within two days. *See pages 114–15 for recipes.*

ALL ITALIAN

❧

A vegetarian and a seafood pasta, followed by ice bowls of ice cream, make a colorful feast for a small buffet party. *Serves 12*

BROCCOLI & PINE NUT FETTUCCINE
A colorful pasta with the sharp flavor of lemon.

SHRIMP & MUSHROOM PAPARDELLE
This dish is delicious in its mix of tastes and textures.

COFFEE & AMARETTO ICE CREAM
The creamy blend of coffee and almond is not too sweet.

DRINKS
A dry sparkling Prosecco from the Veneto would provide just the right splash of vino to complement the pasta. For an extra-special treat, serve sweet Vin Santo with the ice cream – the apricot-flavored variety would be excellent.

PLANNING NOTES
Make the ice cream up to six weeks in advance. Both pasta sauces can be prepared up to eight hours ahead. Quickly heat each one through in the pasta saucepan while the pasta drains in a colander. Pasta tastes best immediately after cooking, but at least it is easy to cook. Toss the pasta back in with the sauce and serve in warmed pasta bowls. The shrimp must be cooked at the last minute. *See pages 116–17 for recipes.*

are happy

CHAMPAGNE BUFFET

A festive trio of elegant dishes that can be prepared in advance for a special occasion. Serves 18

MARINATED SALMON
Home-prepared gravlax with a luscious herbed-mustard sauce.

CHICKEN CREPE STACK
An impressive tower of crepes layered with chicken, ham, and asparagus in a creamy wine sauce.

FRESH FRUIT SAVARIN
A rum-soaked ring of sweet yeast bread filled with fruit soaked in rum and lime.

DRINKS
This is a feast that calls out for Champagne. Before the meal start with Champagne cocktails (see page 135 for recipes), followed by a vintage Champagne with the salmon and the chicken crepe stack. A fine Sauternes makes a superb accompaniment for the savarin.

PLANNING NOTES
Prepare the sauce for the chicken stack up to eight hours in advance, but make the crepes and assemble the stack just before baking. After baking, the stack can be frozen whole for up to six weeks. Defrost fully before heating for 30 minutes in a moderate oven. Make the savarin up to two days (but no more) in advance, as it improves with a day's soaking in its rum syrup. It can be frozen (without syrup) for up to six weeks. Prepare the salmon and its sauce up to three hours in advance and refrigerate. *See pages 118–19 for recipes.*

LUNCHEON

This light buffet would be perfect served on a summer day in glorious dappled shade.
Serves 12

HOMEMADE OAT COOKIES & CHEESE
Crumbly cookies served with a selection of cheeses.

PORK WITH TUNA SAUCE
Eaten cold, this unlikely-sounding combination is exceptionally good.

WEST INDIAN PUNCH GELATIN
An attractive mold with the flavors of exotic fruits and rum.

DRINKS
With the cheeses and the pork, choose a Semillon Chardonnay, and to accompany the gelatin, a sweet Muscat. The orange-flavored Muscat is my particular favorite.

PLANNING NOTES
Bake the cookies a day in advance, and store in an airtight tin. The pork needs to marinate for at least 24 hours, but do not make it more than 36 hours ahead. Prepare the gelatin mold the day before, and keep it in the refrigerator until you are ready to serve. *See pages 120–21 for recipes.*

BIRTHDAY PARTY FOR 18

CASSOULET

35 MINUTES   2 HOURS 55 MINUTES   12 HOURS SOAKING

INGREDIENTS

2½ LB (1.25KG) BONED SHOULDER OF LAMB
2 CUPS (500ML) DRY WHITE WINE
6 ONIONS, COARSELY CHOPPED
8 SPRIGS MARJORAM, PLUS 3 TBSP FRESH
MARJORAM, FINELY CHOPPED (OR 2 TSP DRIED)
2LB (1KG) DRIED WHITE BEANS, SOAKED FOR
12 HOURS, RINSED & DRAINED
¾ LB (375G) SLICED SMOKED PANCETTA
OR BACON
2½ LB (1.25KG) CANNED PLUM TOMATOES
3 LARGE CARROTS, CUT INTO CHUNKS
1 LEMON, ZEST ONLY, CUT INTO THIN STRIPS
4 GARLIC CLOVES, SKINS LEFT ON, CRUSHED
UNDER THE FLAT OF A KNIFE
3 BAY LEAVES
1½ LB (750G) TOULOUSE SAUSAGES
OR COARSE 100% PORK SAUSAGES
1½ LB (750G) DUCK BREASTS, SKINNED
2 TBSP OLIVE OIL (IF FRYING)
SALT & PEPPER TO TASTE
4 CUPS (250G) FRESH WHITE BREAD CRUMBS
4 TBSP FLAT-LEAF PARSLEY, COARSELY CHOPPED
SALAD GREENS TO SERVE

1 Preheat oven to 375°F/190°C. Place the lamb in a large roasting pan with the wine, half the onions, and the marjoram sprigs. Bake in the oven for 2 hours.

2 Meanwhile make the bean mixture: Place the presoaked beans in a large saucepan, cover with lightly salted water, bring to a boil, and boil steadily for 15 minutes. Drain.

3 Return the beans to the pan and add the pancetta, tomatoes, carrots, lemon zest, remaining onions, 3 garlic cloves, and the chopped marjoram and bay leaves. Cover with water, bring to a boil, then simmer, covered, for 1 hour, stirring occasionally.

4 Brown the sausages and duck breasts under the broiler or cook in a large skillet with oil. Add them to the bean and vegetable mixture, cover, and cook over a moderate heat for 30 minutes longer.

5 Remove the saucepan from the heat, then drain, reserving the liquid, but discarding the garlic cloves. Adjust seasoning. Once cool enough to handle, cut the sausages and duck into bite-size chunks.

6 When the lamb is cooked, remove from the oven and let cool. Turn the oven to 350°F/180°C. Trim the lamb of excess fat and cut into bite-size

chunks. Reserve the liquid but discard the onions and marjoram sprigs.

7 Rub the insides of 2 large casseroles with the remaining garlic clove, then arrange the bean and vegetable mixture, sausage, duck, and lamb in alternating layers, finishing with a layer of beans and vegetables. Pour over the wine and juices from the lamb and the reserved liquid from the beans and vegetables.

8 In a small bowl, combine the bread crumbs and parsley. Take half the mixture and sprinkle it over the surface of both casseroles.

9 Bake for 20 minutes, then push the crumbs down into the liquid and sprinkle the remaining bread crumb mixture over each dish. Bake for 45 minutes more (65 minutes total), allowing the layer of bread crumbs to brown. Serve with a green salad.

COOK'S TIPS
In the final dish, the meat and beans should be just moist; you may need to add a little more wine in the last 30 minutes of cooking. You can substitute 1½ lb (750g) canned confit of duck for the duck breasts; as confit is already cooked, add it in Step 7. The dish can be prepared to Step 8 two days in advance, and finished on the day.

CHOCOLATE BIRTHDAY CAKE

30 MINUTES   1 HOUR 50 MINUTES

INGREDIENTS
1¾ LB (875G) SEMISWEET CHOCOLATE
12 LARGE EGGS: 9 SEPARATED, 3 WHOLE
1½ CUPS (375G) SUPERFINE SUGAR
2½ CUPS (300G) GROUND HAZELNUTS
2 TBSP INSTANT COFFEE GRANULES, DISSOLVED
IN 1 TBSP HOT WATER, COOLED
3 TBSP COFFEE LIQUEUR (OPTIONAL)
PINCH OF CREAM OF TARTAR
¾ CUP (175G) UNSALTED BUTTER

COOK'S TIPS
If you are using a microwave, 1lb (500g) of chocolate broken in pieces will take about 6 minutes to melt on medium. The cake can be made a day in advance, and coated on the day it is needed, but it is best eaten within 24 hours. Crystallized Petals or Chocolate Leaves (page 170) can be used instead of fresh petals for decoration.

1 Preheat oven to 350°F/180°C. Break 1lb (500g) of the chocolate into small pieces, then heat in a double boiler, or heatproof bowl over a saucepan of simmering water, or in a microwave. Stir gently (do not beat) as it melts until smooth. Let cool.

2 Whisk the egg yolks, whole eggs, and sugar until pale and fluffy.

3 Gently fold the melted chocolate and ground hazelnuts into the egg mixture, then the cooled coffee and coffee liqueur, if using. In another bowl, whisk the egg whites and cream of tartar until they form stiff peaks, then add them to the cake mixture. Spoon the mixture into a lined and greased 10in (25cm) round cake pan.

4 Bake on the lowest shelf of the oven for 1 hour 20 minutes. Leave the cake in its pan for 10 minutes, and cool on a wire rack.

5 To make the covering, heat the butter and remaining chocolate as in Step 2, stirring very gently until smooth. Let cool for about 5 minutes, so that it thickens slightly.

6 With the cake still upside down, spread the chocolate mixture over the surface of the cake and around the sides. Let the covering set, then transfer to a cake plate and decorate with fresh flower petals.

CHOCOLATE
BIRTHDAY CAKE

ALL ITALIAN FOR 12

BROCCOLI & PINE NUT FETTUCCINE

10 MINUTES 15 MINUTES

INGREDIENTS
2½ LB (1.25KG) BROCCOLI
¾ CUP (175G) BUTTER
24 FRESH SAGE LEAVES, SHREDDED
3 LEMONS, FINELY SLICED FRUIT OF ½,
JUICE & GRATED ZEST OF 2½
2OZ (60G) PICKLED LEMON SLICES (OPTIONAL)
SALT & PEPPER TO TASTE
2LB (1KG) FETTUCCINE
6 TBSP (90G) PINE NUTS, LIGHTLY TOASTED
PARMESAN CHEESE, GRATED FOR TOPPING

1 Trim the broccoli and cut the larger florets in half. Cook in a saucepan of salted boiling water for 3 minutes. Refresh under cold water and drain.

2 Heat the butter in a large skillet until it just begins to brown. Immediately add the broccoli, sage, lemon slices, and pickled lemon (if using). Cook over low heat for 5 minutes, until warmed through, then add the lemon juice and zest. Adjust the seasoning.

3 Cook the fettuccine in 2 large saucepans with plenty of salted boiling water for 6 minutes if dried, 5–6 minutes if fresh, until *al dente*. Drain, then return it to the 2 pans. Add half each of the broccoli mixture and pine nuts to each pan, and toss. Serve immediately, sprinkled with Parmesan.

COOK'S TIP
Use 2 very large saucepans of lightly salted boiling water for the pasta as it needs to be uncrowded when it cooks.

SHRIMP & MUSHROOM PAPARDELLE

30 MINUTES 25 MINUTES

INGREDIENTS
1LB (500G) LARGE SHRIMP
2 CUPS (500ML) WATER
5 TBSP (75ML) OLIVE OIL
4 GARLIC CLOVES, FINELY CHOPPED
6 PLUM TOMATOES, PEELED
& FINELY CHOPPED
3 TBSP TOMATO PASTE
½ LB (250G) BROWN OR SHIITAKE
MUSHROOMS, SLICED
2 TSP GROUND BLACK PEPPER
SALT TO TASTE
2LB (1KG) PAPARDELLE OR FETTUCCINE
1 CUP (250G) MASCARPONE
FRESH BASIL, SHREDDED, TO GARNISH
TOMATO & BASIL SALAD TO SERVE

1 Prepare the shrimp (see Step 1, page 94), reserving shells for stock.

2 To make the stock, crush the shells and place in a large saucepan with the water. Bring to a boil. Simmer for 30 minutes, until reduced by half. Strain and discard the shells.

3 To make the sauce, heat 3 tablespoons of the oil in a large saucepan over moderate heat, then add the garlic. Cook for about 5 minutes, then add the tomatoes and tomato paste. Turn heat to low and cook for about 10 minutes.

4 Add the mushrooms, pepper, and stock. Bring to a boil and simmer for 5 minutes. Add the salt. Keep warm over very low heat.

5 Cook the papardelle in 2 large saucepans with plenty of salted boiling water for 8–10 minutes if dried, 5–6 minutes if fresh, until *al dente*.

6 While the pasta is cooking, heat the remaining oil in a skillet until very hot, then add the shrimp and cook for about 1 minute on each side, until they turn pink.

7 Drain the pasta, then return it to the 2 pans. Add half each of the shrimp sauce and mascarpone to each pan and toss. Garnish with basil and serve with a tomato and basil salad.

SHRIMP &
MUSHROOM
PAPARDELLE

COFFEE & AMARETTO ICE CREAM

☑ 20 MINUTES ☕ 10 MINUTES 🍶 8 HOURS CHILLING

INGREDIENTS

3¾ CUPS (900ML) LIGHT CREAM, CHILLED
1 CUP (250G) SUPERFINE SUGAR
1¼ OZ (35G) INSTANT COFFEE GRANULES
3 CUPS (750ML) CRÈME FRAÎCHE
OR LIGHT SOUR CREAM
1 TBSP VANILLA EXTRACT
2 TSP GROUND NUTMEG
8OZ (250G) AMARETTI COOKIES, CRUSHED
(⅔ COARSELY, ⅓ FINELY)
1 CUP (200ML) MILK
4 TBSP UNSALTED BUTTER
7OZ (200G) SEMISWEET CHOCOLATE,
BROKEN IN SMALL PIECES

1 To make the ice cream, heat ⅔ cup of the cream with the sugar in a saucepan, stirring until the sugar dissolves. Add ½ cup of the coffee. Let cool, then refrigerate for at least 2 hours, until thoroughly chilled.

2 Whisk in the remaining cream, crème fraîche, vanilla, and nutmeg.

3 Turn the mixture into a rigid freezerproof container, cover, and freeze for 3 hours, stirring at the end of each hour (follow the manufacturer's instructions if you use an ice cream

maker). On the final stirring, add the crushed amaretti. Refreeze for 3 hours.

4 To make the sauce, heat the milk and butter in a saucepan and bring to a boil. Remove from the heat, then stir in the remaining coffee and the chocolate. Stir gently until mixed and let cool, stirring occasionally.

5 Transfer the ice cream to the refrigerator 30 minutes before eating to soften. To serve, sprinkle fine amaretti crumbs over the top and pour over the sauce.

CHAMPAGNE BUFFET FOR 18

MARINATED SALMON

20 MINUTES · 2 HOURS 30 MINUTES CHILLING

INGREDIENTS

2LB (1KG) FRESH SALMON, BONED,
SKINNED, & FILLETED
6 LEMONS, JUICE & GRATED ZEST
OF 4, JUICE OF 2
1½ CUPS (350ML) SAFFLOWER OIL OR ANY
OTHER LIGHT OIL
1OZ (30G) FRESH DILL, FINELY CHOPPED,
PLUS SPRIGS TO GARNISH
1½ TSP SALT
½ TSP GROUND BLACK PEPPER
5 TBSP (75G) DIJON MUSTARD
1 TBSP SUPERFINE SUGAR
CAPERS (OPTIONAL), TO GARNISH

1 Chill the salmon in the freezer for about 1 hour 30 minutes, until it is almost frozen. Cut very thin slices diagonally across the grain. Place on a large platter.

2 To make the marinade, combine the juice and grated zest of 4 lemons and ⅔ cup (150ml) of the oil. Add half the chopped dill and 1 teaspoon of salt. Pour over the salmon slices. Sprinkle with pepper and leave, in the refrigerator, covered with plastic wrap, for 1–18 hours.

3 To make the dressing, combine the mustard, juice of 2 lemons, sugar, remaining salt, and remaining chopped dill. Drizzle in remaining oil, a little at a time, beating constantly, or liquidize in a blender until smooth. Garnish each portion with a sprig of dill and capers, if using, and serve with the sauce and brown bread.

COOK'S TIP
If the salmon is well chilled it will slice much more easily. Alternatively, ask your market to slice it for you. Keep it well refrigerated until use.

CHICKEN CREPE STACK

1 HOUR 5 MINUTES · 1 HOUR

INGREDIENTS

4 CUPS (475G) ALL-PURPOSE FLOUR, SIFTED
6 EGGS
10 CUPS (2.8 LITERS) MILK
6 TBSP (90ML) VEGETABLE OIL
2 TBSP FINELY CHOPPED FRESH THYME
SALT & PEPPER TO TASTE
3⅔ CUP (900ML) DRY WHITE WINE
1 CUP (250G) BUTTER
3½ CUPS (475G) GRATED PARMESAN CHEESE
4½ LB (2.25G) COOKED CHICKEN, DICED
1½ LB (750G) COOKED SMOKED HAM, DICED
36 ASPARAGUS SPEARS, COOKED AL DENTE

COOK'S TIPS
Each stack will serve about 6 people, so you will need to make 3 for 18 guests. Once assembled, the stacks can be frozen for 2 months. Defrost, then reheat for 30 minutes in a moderate oven.

1 To make the crepe batter, blend in a food processor 2¼ cups (300g) flour, eggs, 3⅔ cups (900ml) milk, oil, thyme, and seasoning. Beat until well mixed. Refrigerate for 30 minutes.

2 Meanwhile, make the filling. Bring the wine to a boil and reduce by about three-quarters. Add ¾ cup (175g) of the butter and the remaining flour, and mix to a smooth paste. Gradually add the remaining milk, stirring with each addition, until smooth. Cook gently for 15 minutes.

3 Stir in the Parmesan, reserving ¾ cup (90g). Adjust the seasoning, then remove the sauce from the heat. Stir in the chicken and ham. Mix well.

4 Preheat oven to 400°F/200°C. Heat 1 teaspoon of butter in a 9in (23cm) skillet until it just browns. Add 3 tablespoons of batter and cook the crepe on both sides until golden. Repeat until the batter is used, regreasing the pan between crepes.

5 In a 9in (23cm) greased, loose-bottomed cake pan, make the first stack. Lay 1 crepe on the base, then cover it with about 8 tablespoons of filling. Repeat for 6 more layers, adding 6 asparagus spears on 2 of the layers. Finish with a crepe and one-third of the remaining Parmesan. Assemble 2 more stacks. Bake for 30 minutes, allow to cool slightly, turn out, and serve warm.

FRESH FRUIT SAVARIN

20 MINUTES ⏱ 1 HOUR ☐ 1 HOUR 45 MINUTES STANDING

INGREDIENTS

2½ CUPS (575G) SUPERFINE SUGAR
1¼ CUPS (300ML) MILK, WARMED
1 TBSP INSTANT YEAST
4 CUPS (500G) BREAD FLOUR, SIFTED
6 LARGE EGGS, LIGHTLY BEATEN
2 TSP SALT
SCANT 1 CUP (200G) BUTTER, MELTED
2½ CUPS (600ML) WATER
SCANT 1 CUP (200ML) DARK RUM, KIRSCH,
OR BRANDY
EXOTIC OR SEASONAL FRESH FRUIT
CRÈME FRAÎCHE OR HEAVY CREAM TO SERVE

COOK'S TIPS

If you are not using instant yeast, follow the instructions on the yeast packet. If the savarin is browning too quickly in the oven, cover it with waxed paper for the last 10 minutes of cooking. In summer, the savarin is very good served with mixed berries.

1 To make the savarin, place ¼ cup (75g) of the sugar, the warmed milk, yeast, flour, eggs, and salt in a large, greased bowl, and beat well. Cover with plastic wrap and a dish towel, and let stand in a warm place for 1 hour, until doubled in size.

2 On a floured work surface, punch down the dough and knead in the melted butter. Knead for about 10 minutes, until elastic, then place the dough in a greased and floured 12in (30cm) savarin mold. Cover with oiled plastic wrap and let rise in a warm place for 45 minutes more, until it is about level with the top of the pan. Preheat oven to 375°F/190°C.

4 Bake for 45 minutes. Let cool for 30 minutes, then ease it loose from its pan, but do not remove it yet.

5 While the savarin is baking, make the syrup. Place the water and remaining sugar in a saucepan and bring slowly to a boil, stirring until the sugar has dissolved. Boil for 15 minutes; do not allow the syrup to caramelize. Remove from the heat and let cool slightly, then add the rum.

6 Prick the savarin all over with a skewer and drizzle over the syrup, reserving about 1½ cups (300ml), until it is absorbed. When the savarin has cooled completely, place it on an 18in (45cm) serving platter. Fill the center with fresh fruit. Slice and serve with the fruit, a spoonful of syrup, and crème fraîche or heavy cream.

FRESH FRUIT
SAVARIN

LUNCHEON FOR 12

HOMEMADE OAT COOKIES & CHEESE

⏱ 15 MINUTES 🍲 25 MINUTES

INGREDIENTS
1 CUP (125G) PLAIN WHOLE-WHEAT FLOUR,
SIFTED
1¼ CUPS (150G) OAT FLOUR, PLUS
EXTRA FOR DUSTING
1¼ CUPS (150G) OLD-FASHIONED OATMEAL
1½ TSP BAKING POWDER, SIFTED
1 TSP SALT
1 TBSP SUGAR
½ CUP (125G) UNSALTED BUTTER, MELTED

1 In a large mixing bowl, combine the flour, the oat flour, the oatmeal, baking powder, salt, and sugar. Make a well in the center and pour in the melted butter. Mix well.

2 Add the cold water, a little at a time. Knead until well blended and the dough is firm and holds together. Divide the mixture in 2, and sprinkle oat flour all over both pieces.

3 Preheat oven to 325°F/160°C. Line and grease 2 baking sheets. Dust a work surface with oat flour and roll out the first piece of dough to about ⅛ in (3mm) thick.

4 Dust the upper surface with oat flour. With a 2in (5cm) cutter, cut the dough into rounds. Place them ¼ in (5mm) apart on the baking sheet.

5 Repeat for the remaining dough on the second sheet. Bake for 25 minutes, until the cookies are golden, then transfer to a wire rack to cool.

COOK'S TIPS
These crackerlike cookies may be made 2 days in advance and stored in an airtight tin. Choose a mixture of soft and hard cow's milk and goat milk cheeses to serve with the cookies. Make sure that they are brought slowly to room temperature if they have been chilled.

HOMEMADE OAT COOKIES
WITH A SELECTION OF CHEESES
*Clockwise from right: Goat Cheese,
Torta di Dolcelatte, Blue Shropshire,
Goat Cheese, and Brie.*

PORK WITH TUNA SAUCE

20 MINUTES   1 HOUR 45 MINUTES   24 HOURS CHILLING

INGREDIENTS
3 TBSP BUTTER
¼ CUP (350ML) OLIVE OIL
3LB (1.5KG) BONED LOIN OF PORK
SALT & PEPPER TO TASTE
3 CUPS (750ML) MILK
3 BAY LEAVES
⅔ CUP (150ML) CRÈME FRAÎCHE
OR LIGHT SOUR CREAM
1 LEMON, JUICE ONLY
10OZ (300G) CANNED TUNA IN OIL, DRAINED
6 ANCHOVY FILLETS
6 TBSP CAPERS
⅔ CUP (150ML) MAYONNAISE (SEE PAGE 147)
TOMATO & BASIL SALAD TO SERVE

1 Heat the butter and 3 tablespoons of oil in a heavy casserole until the butter has melted. Put in the pork, skin side down. Add the seasoning. Brown well on both sides.

2 Add half of the milk and the bay leaves and bring to a boil, then simmer. Half-cover the pan and cook for 1 hour, turning the pork once. Add the remaining milk. Cover and simmer very gently for 40 minutes more. Remove the pork and let cool, discarding the contents of the pan.

3 Meanwhile, make the sauce. Put the remaining oil, crème fraîche, lemon juice, tuna, anchovies, and capers in a blender and liquidize until smooth. Fold the mixture into the Mayonnaise. Adjust seasoning.

4 Cut the pork into very thin slices. Spread a thin layer of sauce on the bottom of a large serving dish and place a layer of pork slices on top. Repeat until both the pork and sauce are used, finishing with a thin layer of sauce. Cover and refrigerate for 24 hours. Serve cold with a tomato and basil salad.

COOK'S TIP
In Italy, veal is traditionally used to make this dish, and it can be substituted for the pork.

WEST INDIAN PUNCH GELATIN

30 MINUTES   5 MINUTES   5 HOURS CHILLING

INGREDIENTS
3 TBSP POWDERED GELATIN
½ CUP (125ML) WATER
2 CUPS (500ML) ORANGE JUICE
2 CUPS (500ML) PINEAPPLE JUICE
2 CUPS (500ML) MANGO JUICE
½ CUP (125G) SUPERFINE SUGAR
6 LIMES, JUICE ONLY
1 CUP (250ML) WHITE RUM OR GRAPE JUICE
PLUS 1 TBSP RUM EXTRACT
½ TSP GRATED NUTMEG
36 LITCHIS (FRESH OR CANNED),
SKINNED, PITS REMOVED
TROPICAL FRUITS, SLICED, TO SERVE

1 Sprinkle the gelatin onto the water in a small saucepan. Let soak for 5 minutes. Place over very low heat and stir until the gelatin has dissolved and the liquid is clear.

2 In a large saucepan, heat the orange, pineapple, and mango juices with the sugar, stirring gently until the sugar has dissolved.

3 Bring the liquid almost to a boil and add the gelatin. Stir well to mix. Reserve 2 tablespoons of the lime juice; add the remainder with the rum and nutmeg to the pan. Stir again.

4 Rinse 12 individual 1 cup (250ml) molds (or 2 x 1 quart (1 liter) molds) in cold water, then half-fill each, using only half of the mixture. Let cool, then refrigerate for 1½ hours. Let the remaining mixture stand at room temperature.

5 Place 3 litchis in the center of each mold on top of the gelatin, then top up with the remaining mixture. Refrigerate for at least 5 hours (but best overnight). Serve with tropical fruits sprinkled with the reserved lime juice.

COOK'S TIPS
Serve straight from the refrigerator the day after it is made for best results. To loosen the gelatin in its mold, place the mold in lukewarm water almost up to the rim for about 1 minute before unmolding. The gelatin can also be made in a loaf terrine and cut into slices before serving.

COCKTAIL PARTIES

DEVILISH DRINKS SERVED IN ELEGANT GLASSES WITH PLATTERS OF DELECTABLE SAVORIES, ALL AGAINST AN IMPRESSIVE BACKDROP OF HIGHLY POLISHED SILVERWARE AND EXQUISITE FLOWERS: THESE ARE THE EXCITING ELEMENTS THAT MAKE UP THAT MOST GLAMOROUS OF OCCASIONS, THE COCKTAIL PARTY. THIS SHOULD NOT BE A TIME TO HOLD BACK: FOR A SENSATION-PACKED EVENT, MAKE SURE THAT YOU PULL OUT ALL THE STOPS.

Create a thrilling atmosphere with bold arrangements of flowers (right), wickedly indulgent drinks, and imaginative food from the cocktail menu (page 128).

GLAMOUR

"I can resist everything except temptation."

LIVELY PRESENTATION with a sophisticated atmosphere will guarantee that both old-time favorites and exotic delicacies are impossible to resist.

FLOWERS AND CANDLES

A low arrangement becomes even more effective when it includes candles. For safety, be sure the lit candles are taller than any plant material in the basket.

Ranunculus

Snapdragon

Tulip

Rose

Orchid

Ivy

1 Line a basket, or other low container, with plastic. Place the candles and secure with clay. Fill the basket with soaked florists' foam, cutting it to fit around the candles. Place trailing foliage, such as ivy, around the edges.

2 Cut the flower stems to 2½ in (6cm). Insert them so they protrude about 1in (2.5cm) above the edge of the container. Arrange them in bands of color, as the roses are here.

3 Keep the color bands quite informal and fill in gaps with "pools" of flowers, hiding all the foam and plastic to complete the arrangement (above right).

OSCAR WILDE 1854–1900

DRINK TRAY
A polished silver tray reflects the glasses and their exciting contents, showing them off to great advantage.

BOLD PLATTER
Brilliant red plates echo the vibrant colors of some of the cocktails, the food, and the basket of flowers.

COCKTAIL NAPKINS
When eating finger food, small napkins (linen for greatest luxury) are essential. Arrange a pile on the table within easy reach.

THE CHANCE TO IMPRESS

AN ELEGANT ARRANGEMENT

Flowers always play a key role in creating atmosphere, but they are especially important at cocktail or buffet parties where there is no formal seating plan. Position arrangements where they can be seen easily among your guests. Make use of side tables, cabinet tops, or wide mantelpieces and, in summer, place one or more arrangements on garden tables outdoors.

Astilbe

Rose

1 ◁ Wedge chicken wire or soaked florists' foam into a container. Insert stout-stemmed plants, such as the viburnum here, in a fanlike shape; make it balanced but not too formal.

2 ▷ Add the largest blooms, here highly scented white lilies, balancing them within the arrangement. Remove the pollen sacs, which might stain guests' clothing.

3 ◁ Fill in with the remaining flowers: feathery white astilbe, ice-blue delphiniums, and orange roses to tie in with the flower basket on pages 124–25. Then, assess the arrangement from a distance, inserting more material as necessary until you achieve the final effect (right).

Viburnum

Delphinium

Lily

IMPORTANT ELEMENTS
Begin with a plant that has quite rigid stems to form the framework, add something bold to give balance, and then fill in with softer flowers.

A WINNING COMBINATION
The marriage of container and flowers is an important one. This display is shown off to perfection in the flowing silhouette of a Champagne cooler.

FROSTED COCKTAILS

Merry Melon and Touch of the Blues, here, are just two of many colorful cocktails that will look very attractive with a salt or sugar edging on the glass. See pages 134–37 for the drink recipes.

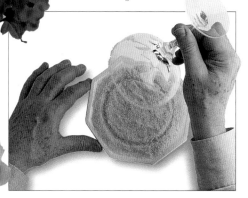

1 Mix 2–3 drops of food coloring into 4 tablespoons of sugar to produce a colored edging. Moisten the rim of a glass with lime juice or water and gently dip it into a plate of the sugar or table salt.

2 If the crystals on the rim are too large, clean the glass and begin again. Pour the cocktail carefully into the glass.

For a white edging use table salt or sugar

MENUS
"Cocktails are society's most enduring

COCKTAIL FOOD

These bite-sized delicacies are easy to eat: essential when guests are standing and holding a glass, too. Serve the food from a tray so the toothpicks can be disposed of immediately and discreetly.

COCKTAIL KEBABS
Tiny kebabs of shrimp, scallops, artichokes, asparagus, red pepper, mushrooms, and baby corn, all wrapped in prosciutto and grilled.

PHYLLO BUNDLES
These miniature purses have a distinctly North African flavor. Ricotta forms the base for all three fillings:
CHICKEN & APRICOT *with walnut.*
CURRANT & PINE NUT *with cinnamon.*
ARTICHOKE *with ginger and marjoram.*

FRUITS WITH PROSCIUTTO
Firm but sweet chunks of papaya, mango, fig, and melon are rolled up in delicate strips of prosciutto.

CROSTINI
Crisp toasted baguette with a choice of scrumptious toppings:
MUSHROOM *cooked in red wine, with pecans and nutmeg.*
MEDITERRANEAN *mix of tomatoes, olives, capers, and herbs.*
TOMATO & BASIL, *a traditional combination that never fails to please.*

SUSHI
Bites of rice, fish, and vegetables that taste as good as they look.
SALMON BALLS, *smoked salmon encircling delicate spheres of sushi rice.*
NORI ROLLS, *spirals of seaweed filled with rice, vegetables, and fish.*
ROE BOATS, *seaweed-wrapped rice, topped with caviar or lumpfish roe.*

PLANNING NOTES
The crostini toppings and the phyllo bundles can be cooked and frozen six weeks ahead, or made and refrigerated the day before; the crostini bases are best fresh. The sushi, fruits in prosciutto, and the kebabs (up to their grilling) can be prepared up to eight hours in advance and kept refrigerated. Cover the crostini bases with topping, and heat these, the phyllo bundles, and the kebabs for six to eight minutes in a moderate oven just before serving. The hot food is best fresh, so enlist help in the kitchen if you can. *See pages 130–33 for recipes.*

invention." ELSA MAXWELL 1883–1963

COCKTAIL DRINKS

Beware! These rapturous alcoholic drinks (listed below according to their base) are quite strong. Fortunately, the non-alcoholic punches are tempting and delicious, too.

TEQUILA
MARGARITA • FROZEN MARGARITA
MERRY MELON • TEQUILA SUNRISE

VODKA
BLACK & JADE • SEA BREEZE
VODKA MARTINI

WHISKEY
WHISKEY SOUR • SCOTCH MIST

BRANDY
MINT JULEP • SIDECAR

GIN
TOM COLLINS • PERFECT MARTINI
NEGRONI

RUM
PIÑA COLADA • DAIQUIRI
TOUCH OF THE BLUES • MY RUM PUNCH

CHAMPAGNE
CHAMPAGNE COCKTAIL • PIMM'S ROYAL
BLACK VELVET

NONALCOHOLIC PUNCHES
CRANBERRY • ORANGE
GRAPEFRUIT • APPLE

PLANNING NOTES
Select a maximum of three cocktails and two nonalcoholic punches for your party; more than this will be difficult to manage, as the cocktails cannot be mixed ahead. Making drinks for a crowd is a busy job. You will need a full-time bartender for a large party. Equip your bartender with a cocktail shaker, knives for cutting citrus fruits, a stirring spoon, and a strainer. Noncarbonated bases for cocktails and punches can be made in advance, then shaken with ice or mixed with the other chilled or carbonated ingredients. *See pages 134–37 for recipes.*

COCKTAIL FOOD 1

COCKTAIL KEBABS

🍴 30 MINUTES 🍲 15 MINUTES ☐ 1 HOUR SOAKING

INGREDIENTS FOR 24 KEBABS
12 SPEARS OF MINIATURE ASPARAGUS
½ RED PEPPER, CORED & SEEDED
8 SLICES OF PROSCIUTTO, CUT VERY THIN
4 BABY CORNS
5 JUMBO SHRIMP, PEELED
5 BITE-SIZED SCALLOPS
24 TOOTHPICKS, SOAKED IN
WATER FOR 1 HOUR
4 TBSP BUTTER, MELTED
6 BUTTON MUSHROOMS
3 CANNED ARTICHOKE HEARTS, HALVED

1 Preheat broiler to medium. Blanch the asparagus in a saucepan of simmering, lightly salted water for 3–4 minutes, until *al dente*. Refresh in cold water, drain, then pat dry.

2 Cut the pepper into 6 long strips, about ½ in (1cm) thick.

3 Cut the prosciutto into 24 strips, about 5 x 1in (12 x 2.5cm), then use them to wrap individual ears of corn, shrimp, and scallops, securing each kebab with a toothpick. Brush with melted butter and grill for about 2 minutes on each side, until the shrimps have turned pink and the prosciutto just begins to brown.

4 Wrap three spears of asparagus in a piece of prosciutto and secure with a toothpick. Repeat to make 3 more asparagus kebabs in the same way. Brush with butter and broil for about 1 minute on each side, until the prosciutto begins to brown.

5 Wrap each mushroom in a strip of prosciutto and spear individually onto a toothpick with a piece of artichoke and a slice of pepper. Brush with melted butter and broil for about 3 minutes on each side, until browned.

COOK'S TIPS
The kebabs can be cooked in advance, kept refrigerated, and then heated in the oven at 350°F/180°C for about 6 minutes before serving.

NOTES ON QUANTITIES
Allow up to eight canapés per person if you are serving them at a cocktail party, or three to five per person as premeal nibbles or a small appetizer. You may need fewer of the more filling ones, such as the crostini. The quantities for all recipes can be reduced or increased as necessary. The crostini bases, sushi rice, and phyllo dough will provide enough for 72 canapés; reduce the amounts proportionately if you are making only one or two of the toppings or fillings. I would suggest preparing only one or two dishes for your party; the sushi, for instance, can be sufficient on its own.

FRUITS WITH
PROSCIUTTO

PHYLLO BUNDLES
🥄 30 MINUTES 🍳 10 MINUTES

INGREDIENTS FOR 72 BUNDLES
12 SHEETS PHYLLO DOUGH, APPROXIMATELY
12 X 7IN (30 X 17CM)
6 TBSP (90G) BUTTER, MELTED
FILLING OF YOUR CHOICE (SEE BELOW)

1 Preheat oven to 375°F/190°C. Cut the phyllo dough widthwise into 3 sections, about 4in (10cm) wide, then halve each strip to make 72 squares.

2 Brush each square with melted butter and place 1½ teaspoons of the filling of your choice in the center. Gather the corners of the pastry around the filling and twist them together to form a bundle.

3 Place on a greased baking sheet and bake for 8–10 minutes, until crisp and golden.

COOK'S TIPS
Preparation and cooking times refer only to the assembling and baking of the bundles. Keep phyllo dough tightly wrapped or damp while using it. The bundles can be cooked and frozen for up to 6 weeks in advance. Defrost and heat in the oven at 350°F/180°C for about 6 minutes.

CHICKEN & APRICOT

INGREDIENTS FOR 24 BUNDLES
⅔ CUP (150G) RICOTTA
¼ LB (125G) COOKED CHICKEN,
FINELY CHOPPED
½ CUP (60G) DRIED APRICOTS, FINELY CHOPPED
½ CUP (60G) WALNUTS, TOASTED
& FINELY CHOPPED
4 SCALLIONS, FINELY CHOPPED
2 TSP FRESH THYME, FINELY CHOPPED
SALT & PEPPER TO TASTE

Mix all the ingredients together in a large bowl.

CURRANT & PINE NUT

INGREDIENTS FOR 24 BUNDLES
½ CUP (60G) CURRANTS
6 TBSP (90ML) DRY WHITE WINE
⅔ CUP (150G) RICOTTA
½ CUP (60G) PINE NUTS, TOASTED
½ TSP GROUND CINNAMON
SALT & PEPPER TO TASTE

Soak the currants in the wine overnight. Drain them well and mix with the remainder of the ingredients.

ARTICHOKE

INGREDIENTS FOR 24 BUNDLES
⅔ CUP (150G) RICOTTA
4 CANNED ARTICHOKE HEARTS, FINELY CHOPPED
2 TSP FRESH MARJORAM, FINELY CHOPPED
4 SCALLIONS, FINELY CHOPPED
½ TSP GROUND GINGER
SALT & PEPPER TO TASTE

Mix all the ingredients together in a large bowl.

FRUITS WITH PROSCIUTTO
🥄 15 MINUTES

INGREDIENTS FOR 24 ITEMS
1 RIPE MANGO
½ SMALL MELON, SEEDED
2 FIGS
12 THIN SLICES OF PROSCIUTTO, CUT IN HALF
24 TOOTHPICKS

1 Peel the mango and remove the flesh, cutting parallel to the flat side of the pit. Cut the flesh into 8 large chunks. Cut the melon flesh into 8 chunks, or scoop out 8 balls with a melon baller. Cut the figs into quarters.

2 Wrap a piece of prosciutto around each melon chunk and each piece of fig, securing it with a toothpick.

3 Secure a folded piece of ham on top of each mango chunk using a toothpick.

COOK'S TIPS
Other types of ham, thinly sliced, and different fruits, like large strawberries or pear wedges, can also be used. This recipe can easily be doubled to make 48 wrapped fruits, or halved to make 12.

COCKTAIL FOOD 2

CROSTINI

🥄 10 MINUTES 🍲 7 MINUTES

INGREDIENTS FOR 36 ITEMS
2 LARGE BAGUETTES, EACH CUT INTO 18 SLICES
½ IN (1CM) THICK
9 TBSP (135ML) OLIVE OIL
2 GARLIC CLOVES (OPTIONAL)
SALT TO TASTE

1 Preheat oven to 425°F/220°C. Brush both sides of each slice of bread with oil, rub with garlic, if using, and sprinkle with salt.

2 Bake for 7 minutes until each slice is crisp and golden. Pile on your chosen topping, and serve immediately.

COOK'S TIPS
Preparation and cooking times refer to crisping the bases and adding the topping only. The bases are best eaten when fresh, but the toppings can be frozen or made up to 8 hours ahead. Just before serving, cover the bases with topping and heat in the oven at 400°F/200°C for 8 minutes, until crisp.

MUSHROOM

INGREDIENTS FOR 12 ITEMS
1 TBSP OLIVE OIL
½ LB (250G) SHIITAKE MUSHROOMS, SLICED
SCANT 1 CUP (200ML) RED WINE
⅔ CUP (150ML) HEAVY CREAM
¼ TSP GROUND NUTMEG
½ CUP (60G) PECAN HALVES, LIGHTLY TOASTED

Heat the olive oil in a frying pan, add the mushrooms, and cook for about 4 minutes, until they begin to soften. Add the red wine, then reduce until it has almost evaporated.

Stir in the cream, then reduce to a very thick sauce. Remove from the heat and sprinkle on the nutmeg.

Spread on the crostini bases, prepared as above. Garnish with pecan halves.

MEDITERRANEAN

INGREDIENTS FOR 12 ITEMS
3 TBSP OLIVE OIL
3OZ (90G) BOTTLED SUNDRIED TOMATOES, DRAINED & DICED
1 RED PEPPER, SEEDED & CHOPPED
1 TBSP CAPERS, CHOPPED
1 GARLIC CLOVE, FINELY CHOPPED
1 TBSP FRESH OREGANO, FINELY CHOPPED, PLUS SPRIGS TO GARNISH
2 TSP BALSAMIC VINEGAR
1 TSP SUGAR
¾ CUP (90G) GREEN OLIVES, PITTED

Heat the olive oil in a frying pan, add the tomatoes, red pepper, capers, garlic, oregano, vinegar, sugar, and olives. Cook over medium heat for 7 minutes.

Spread on the crostini bases, prepared as above. Garnish each slice with a sprig of oregano.

TOMATO & BASIL

INGREDIENTS FOR 12 ITEMS
1LB (500G) FRESH PLUM TOMATOES
1 TBSP OLIVE OIL
SALT TO TASTE
12 BASIL LEAVES, PLUS 4 TBSP FRESH BASIL, FINELY CHOPPED
2 TBSP PINE NUTS, LIGHTLY TOASTED

Preheat oven to 400°F/200°C. Cut the tomatoes in half lengthwise and place, cut side up, on waxed paper on a baking sheet. Brush the cut surfaces of the tomatoes with olive oil. Sprinkle with salt and bake for 1 hour.

Place a basil leaf on each prepared crostini base, then top with a tomato half. Sprinkle with pine nuts and the chopped basil.

SUSHI

🍲 12 MINUTES 🍶 1 HOUR COOLING

INGREDIENTS FOR 72 ITEMS
2 CUPS (425G) SUSHI RICE
4 CUPS (1 LITER) WATER
1¼ CUPS (200ML) WHITE WINE VINEGAR
½ CUP (60G) CONFECTIONERS' SUGAR
8 GARLIC CLOVES, FINELY CHOPPED
4 X 2IN (5CM) PIECES OF FRESH GINGER,
FINELY CHOPPED
PINCH OF SALT

SUSHI
Clockwise from the top: Salmon Balls, Nori Rolls, and Roe Boats

1 Place the rice and water in a large saucepan, cover, and bring to a boil. Simmer, keeping the pan covered, for about 12 minutes, until the rice has absorbed all the water and is sticky. If you cook half or a third of the rice it will still need 12 minutes cooking time.

2 Remove from the heat and immediately stir in the remaining ingredients. Let stand cooked for at least 50 minutes. When cold, it is ready for shaping. Divide it into portions as required for the sushi recipes below.

COOK'S TIPS
If you do not wish to make all 3 types of sushi, divide it proportionately and cook. Cooking and cooling times refer to preparing only the rice.

SALMON BALLS

INGREDIENTS FOR 24 ITEMS
9OZ (275G) SMOKED SALMON, CUT INTO
24 X 3IN (8CM) SQUARES
2 CUPS (300G) SUSHI RICE
CHIVE LEAVES TO GARNISH

Lay a square of salmon onto a sheet of plastic wrap. Place a small 1in (2.5cm) ball of rice, prepared as above, in the center of the square and use the plastic wrap to draw up the salmon around the ball. Pull up the plastic tightly to make a salmon-covered sphere. Repeat the process to make 24 balls. Refrigerate for about 4 hours, until firm, then decorate the top with chives.

NORI ROLLS

INGREDIENTS FOR 24 ITEMS
4 SHEETS OF ROASTED SEAWEED SUSHI NORI
4 CUPS (700G) SUSHI RICE
¼ LB (125G) VEGETABLES (SCALLIONS,
CHIVES, FINE GREEN BEANS, FINE STRIPS OF
ZUCCHINIS, BABY CARROTS, OR PEPPERS)
½ LB (250G) FISH (COOKED SHRIMP, RED OR
BLACK ROE, FINE STRIPS OF SMOKED SALMON,
RAW TUNA, RAW SALMON, OR RAW SCALLOP)

Place an 8 x 7in (20 x 18cm) sheet of nori (shiny side down) onto plastic wrap. Mist with water to soften. Spread a thin layer of rice, prepared as above, over the nori, leaving a 1in (2.5cm) border along the two long edges.

Lay thin strips of vegetables and fish lengthwise along one end of the rice. Mist the exposed nori edges and roll up lengthwise, using the plastic wrap to help you. Wrap the roll in the plastic and refrigerate for about 4 hours, until firm. Cut each roll into 6 slices, 1in (2.5cm) thick, then remove the wrap.

ROE BOATS

INGREDIENTS FOR 24 ITEMS
2 CUPS (300G) SUSHI RICE
4 SHEETS OF ROASTED SEAWEED SUSHI NORI,
EACH CUT INTO 6 STRIPS
6 TSP BLACK LUMPFISH ROE

Squeeze the rice, prepared as above, into 24 boat-shaped ovals, 1 x ½in (2.5 x 1cm). Mist the strips of nori, then shape each one around a rice boat, pinching the ends together. Refrigerate for about 4 hours, until firm, then fill each boat with ¼ teaspoon of roe.

COCKTAILS 1

TEQUILA BASE
FOR 1 GLASS

MARGARITA

1 SMALL LIME, JUICE ONLY
SALT
2FL OZ (60ML) TEQUILA
4 TSP TRIPLE SEC
ICE CUBES

Rub the rim of a cocktail glass with lime juice then dip in salt to give a fine coated rim. Shake the spirits and remaining lime juice with the ice then strain the liquid into the glass.

FROZEN MARGARITA

1 SMALL LIME, JUICE ONLY
SALT
2FL OZ (60ML) TEQUILA
4 TSP TRIPLE SEC
17FL OZ (500ML) ICE CUBES

Rub the rim of a cocktail glass with lime juice, then dip in salt to give a coated rim. Place the ice in a blender. Pour in the spirits and remaining lime juice and blend for about 10 seconds until slushy. Scoop into the glass.

MERRY MELON

¼ SMALL MELON, SEEDED
½ LEMON, JUICE ONLY
2FL OZ (60ML) TEQUILA
4 TSP GALLIANO
DROP VANILLA EXTRACT
ICE CUBES

In a food processor, pulp the melon flesh. Mix in the remaining ingredients. Shake with the ice for 15 seconds, then strain into a chilled cocktail glass.

TEQUILA SUNRISE

ICE CUBES
1 WEDGE OF LIME
2FL OZ (60ML) TEQUILA
1 ORANGE, JUICE ONLY
DASH OF GRENADINE
¼ PT (150ML) SODA WATER

Half-fill a large highball glass with ice, squeeze the lime wedge over it and drop it in. Add the tequila, orange, and grenadine, and top off with soda.

BARTENDER'S NOTES
As cocktails are high in alcohol, I would allow only two or three drinks per person. You will need a bartender to prepare the drinks for 12 or more guests. Choose only two or three alcoholic cocktails and at least one soft punch. Where quantities make single drinks, multiply for larger numbers. The basic ingredients, excluding ice and any mixers, can be combined in advance and kept chilled. Shake or pour over ice and add any mixers when you serve.

MINT
JULEP

SEA
BREEZE

FROZEN
MARGARITA

VODKA BASE
For 1 Glass

BLACK & JADE

2 FL OZ (50ML) BLACKCURRANT VODKA
1 TSP CRÈME DE MURE OR CASSIS
1 TSP BLUE CURAÇAO
2 BLACKBERRIES OR 5 BLACKCURRANTS
ICE CUBES

Mix the spirits together. Place 2 blackberries or 5 blackcurrants in a chilled cocktail glass. Shake the liquid with ice for 15 seconds, then pour it over the fruit.

SEA BREEZE

2 FL OZ (60ML) VODKA
2 FL OZ (60ML) GRAPEFRUIT JUICE
4 FL OZ (125ML) CRANBERRY JUICE
ICE CUBES

Shake the vodka and fruit juices over the ice, then strain the liquid into a large highball glass.

VODKA MARTINI

1 TSP NOILLY PRAT, CHILLED
2 FL OZ (60ML) VODKA, CHILLED
LEMON TWIST OR GREEN OLIVE

Pour the Noilly Prat into a chilled martini glass, twirl the glass to coat it, then pour the remainder back into the bottle. Swirl the vodka into the glass and add the lemon twist or olive.

WHISKEY BASE
For 1 Glass

WHISKEY SOUR

2 FL OZ (60ML) BOURBON
½ TSP CONFECTIONERS' SUGAR
½ LEMON, JUICE ONLY
2 MARASCHINO CHERRIES
ICE CUBES

Shake the bourbon, sugar, and lemon juice with the ice cubes and strain into a sour glass. Add the cherries.

SCOTCH MIST

2 FL OZ (60ML) SCOTCH
1 FL OZ (30ML) DRY VERMOUTH
½ TSP CONFECTIONERS' SUGAR
1 EGG, ½ WHITE ONLY
ICE CUBES

Shake the Scotch, vermouth, sugar, and half egg white with the ice cubes and strain into a cocktail glass.

BLACK
& JADE

BRANDY BASE
For 1 Glass

MINT JULEP

2 SUGAR CUBES
2 SPRIGS OF MINT
ICE CUBES, CRUSHED
2 FL OZ (60ML) BRANDY OR BOURBON
3 TSP PEACH BRANDY

Rub the sugar cubes with mint leaves and place in a large highball glass. Half-fill with ice, then pour on the brandies. Stir well and top with a sprig of mint.

SIDECAR

2 FL OZ (60ML) BRANDY
4 TSP TRIPLE SEC
½ LEMON, JUICE ONLY
ICE CUBES

Shake the spirits and lemon juice with ice cubes, then strain into a chilled cocktail glass.

COCKTAILS 2

GIN BASE
FOR 1 GLASS

TOM COLLINS

ICE CUBES
2 FL OZ (60ML) GIN
½ LEMON, JUICE ONLY
½ OZ (15G) SUGAR SYRUP
¼ PT (150ML) SODA WATER
TWIST OF LEMON
1 MARASCHINO CHERRY

Half-fill a Collins glass with ice cubes.
Stir in the gin, lemon juice, and sugar
syrup. Top off with soda water, add the
lemon, and decorate with a cherry.

PERFECT MARTINI

1 TSP NOILLY PRAT, CHILLED
2 FL OZ (60ML) GIN, CHILLED
TWIST OF LEMON OR GREEN OLIVE

Pour the Noilly Prat into a chilled
martini glass, twirl the glass to coat it,
then return the rest to the bottle. Pour
in the gin and add the twist of lemon.

NEGRONI

ICE CUBES
2 FL OZ (60ML) GIN
3 TSP SWEET RED VERMOUTH
4 TSP CAMPARI
TWIST OF ORANGE

Half-fill an aperitif glass with ice and
stir in the gin, vermouth, and Campari.
Add the twist of orange.

RUM BASE
FOR 1 GLASS

PIÑA COLADA

3½ FL OZ (100ML) CRUSHED ICE
2 FL OZ (60ML) PALE GOLDEN RUM
1½ FL OZ (45ML) COCONUT CREAM
3 FL OZ (90ML) PINEAPPLE JUICE

Mix all the ingredients in a blender
and pour into a Collins glass.

TOUCH OF THE BLUES

ICE CUBES
1 FL OZ (30ML) WHITE RUM
2 TSP BLUE CURAÇAO
½ LIME, JUICE ONLY
2 TSP KIRSCH
PINCH OF GROUND NUTMEG

Shake all the liquid ingredients with
the ice cubes then strain into a cocktail
glass. Sprinkle with nutmeg.

DAIQUIRI

2 FL OZ (60ML) PALE GOLDEN RUM
4 TSP LIME JUICE
1 TSP SUGAR SYRUP
ICE CUBES

Shake the rum, syrup, and lime with
ice. Strain into a chilled cocktail glass.

MY RUM PUNCH

ICE CUBES
2 FL OZ (60ML) GOLDEN RUM
1 LIME, JUICE ONLY
1 PASSION FRUIT, JUICE ONLY
¼ PT (150ML) PINEAPPLE JUICE, CHILLED
PINCH OF GROUND NUTMEG

Half-fill a highball glass with ice
and stir in the rum and fruit juices.
Sprinkle with nutmeg.

PIÑA COLADA

PIMM'S ROYAL

CHAMPAGNE BASE

FOR 1 GLASS

CHAMPAGNE COCKTAIL

1 SUGAR CUBE
½ TSP ANGOSTURA BITTERS
8FL OZ (250ML) CHAMPAGNE
THIN WEDGE OF ORANGE
TWIST OF LEMON

Place the sugar cube at the bottom of a Champagne flute and shake on the angostura bitters. Pour over the Champagne, then add the wedge of orange and the twist of lemon.

PIMM'S ROYAL

ICE CUBES
2FL OZ (60ML) PIMM'S NO 1
2 SLICES OF CUCUMBER
1 WEDGE OF LEMON
SPRIG OF MINT
6FL OZ (175ML) CHAMPAGNE, CHILLED

Half-fill a large highball glass with ice cubes and pour over the Pimm's. Add the cucumber, wedge of lemon, and the sprig of mint, then top off with chilled Champagne.

BLACK VELVET

4FL OZ (125ML) GUINNESS STOUT, CHILLED
4FL OZ (125ML) CHAMPAGNE, CHILLED

Pour the Guinness into a Champagne flute, then top off with Champagne.

NONALCOHOLIC PUNCHES

FOR 24 GLASSES

CRANBERRY

3 QUARTS (3 LITERS) CRANBERRY JUICE
12 LEMONS, JUICE ONLY
1 QUART (1 LITER) COLD HIBISCUS TEA
2 QUARTS (2 LITERS) GINGER ALE, CHILLED

Mix the fruit juices and tea together and chill. Serve in highball glasses over ice, topped off with ginger ale.

ORANGE

2 QUARTS (2 LITERS) FRESH ORANGE JUICE
12 LIMES, JUICE ONLY
8 TSP ANGOSTURA BITTERS
4 QUARTS (4 LITERS) FIZZY LEMONADE, CHILLED

Mix the fruit juices and bitters together and chill. Serve in highball glasses over ice, topped off with fizzy lemonade.

GRAPEFRUIT

2 QUARTS (2 LITERS) PINK GRAPEFRUIT JUICE
3 QUARTS (3 LITERS) FIZZY LEMONADE
1 CUP (250ML) ELDERFLOWER CORDIAL
12 LEMONS, JUICE ONLY
1¼ PT (750ML) GINGER ALE, CHILLED

Mix the first four ingredients together and chill. Serve in highball glasses over ice, topped off with ginger ale.

APPLE

3 QUARTS (3 LITERS) APPLE JUICE
12 LEMONS, JUICE ONLY
1 QUART (1 LITER) PINEAPPLE JUICE
1 QUART (1 LITER) SODA WATER, CHILLED

Mix the first three ingredients together and chill. Serve in highball glasses over ice, topped off with soda water.

BLACK VELVET

137

BARBECUES

FEW SENSATIONS SET OUR TASTE BUDS TINGLING LIKE THE WONDERFUL AROMA OF OUTDOOR COOKING AND THE UNIQUE FLAVOR OF A BARBECUED MEAL. GLOWING WOOD AND COALS COOK MANY FOODS SUPERBLY. ADD TO THIS THE DELIGHT OF ALFRESCO LUNCHES ON WARM SUMMER DAYS OR EVENING ENTERTAINING UNDER A STARLIT SKY AND, LIKE ME, YOU WILL BE BARBECUING MORE AND MORE, SOMETIMES EVEN IN THE MIDDLE OF WINTER.

Enjoy the dishes of the Seafood Grill menu (page 144) by moon and lantern light (right). All fish and seafood cook extremely well on the barbecue.

MOONLIT
The smoky blue of a moonlit night cut by

MANY OF THE EVENING MEALS I remember most fondly are ones eaten outside, with flickering lanterns, the velvet night sky above, and enticing scents and flavors of food cooked over an aromatic wood fire.

SCENTED CANDLES

Frequently, the scented candles you can buy have a rather synthetic perfume. A simple way to make your own for outside use is to drip five drops of essential oil onto the melted wax around the wick of a burning candle. Citronella and rosemary oil are good for deterring insects.

Use a dropper to drop in the oil

Take care not to drop oil on your hands

MARBLED LANTERNS

Cover the outside of jam or storage jars with marbled paper (see page 70), and use them as sheltered candle holders.

1 On the back of a sheet of paper large enough to entirely encircle the jar, mark a line about 1in (2.5cm) above the jar's top.

3 Wrap the paper around the jar, attaching it to the glass with two-sided tape. Use a long taper to light the candle.

2 Cut out triangles from the top of the paper down to the line. Below the line, cut a pattern of moons and stars through which the light can shine.

Insert the candle first; anchor with putty if necessary

sparkling stars

FLOWERS
The colors of this moonlit theme are echoed in the blue-green medley of ferns, delphiniums, bells of Ireland, and euphorbia.

PAPER LANTERNS
For candlelight lanterns, make or buy marbled paper in appropriate colors.

NAPKINS
Fold each napkin into a triangle, then fold the top of the triangle over.

TUMBLER LIGHTS
Night-light candles in tumblers that shield them from evening breezes are both practical and appealing.

DAYTIME
Simple country food is best in the open air

MAKE SIMPLICITY your goal when setting the table outside for a lunchtime barbecue. Concentrate on comfort and relaxed informality.

INSTANT WINDOW BOX

Fill a wooden box with small potted plants and cut flowers. Use miniature roses in pots as the backbone, and fill in with cut flowers such as these anemones, sweet peas, and pittosporum.

FLOWER NAPKIN RING
Tuck a bold flower between each napkin and its ring. Choose blooms that do not wilt quickly.

1 Completely line a wooden box with a plastic trash bag. Wrap and tape up the rose pots, too, to prevent their roots from becoming waterlogged.

2 Place the pots in first, then wedge in soaked florists' foam, carved to fit around the plastic covered pots. Trim overlapping plastic.

3 Insert the other flowers and foliage into the foam around the roses, keeping the stems fairly upright to simulate natural growth. Be sure the foam is hidden (see finished box above). To prolong the display, replace wilted flowers, and keep foam moist.

FINGER BOWL
A bowl of warm water with citrus slices for finger-dipping is a thoughtful gesture beside each setting at a barbecue.

BEAUTIFUL FLOWERS
Brighten up the table with a simple earthenware vase of flowers that echo the ones in the window box.

MENUS

A glowing, aromatic fire that perfumes food

SEAFOOD GRILL

Nothing beats the flavor of the freshest fish, cooked simply over a wood fire. *Serves 12*

CHARRED SQUID
Fragrant with a wild herb marinade, squid is always a delectable treat.

RED MULLET WITH FENNEL & ORANGE
Fennel enhances most white fish, and none better than the red mullet.

PEPPERED PINEAPPLE
Don't be alarmed by the idea of fruit and pepper. As with strawberries, the peppercorns intensify the fruit's flavor.

DRINKS
A crisp, sharp Chablis has the strength to combine superbly with the nutty, smoky tastes of the fish. A Bourgogne Aligote would also complement the menu.

PLANNING NOTES
Mayonnaise for the mullet will keep for three days in the refrigerator. The marinade for the squid can be made the day before; allow up to four hours for the squid to marinate. Slice the pineapple and squeeze lemon over it to prevent discoloration up to two hours before serving. A second wire grill for your barbecue will save scrubbing between courses.
See pages 146–47 for recipes.

GOURMET BARBECUE

Don't cook only everyday food on a barbecue. Some of the best dishes I have ever eaten were prepared over wood fires. *Serves 6*

TEA-SMOKED TUNA
Sliced tuna, lightly smoked over tea leaves, is a delicacy to be savored.

CRISPY CHICKEN LIVERS
Delicious chicken livers are golden toasty-crisp on the outside and blush pink on the inside.

ROASTED PLANTAINS WITH RUM SAUCE
Ripe plantain, caramelized on the fire, with a sauce that transports you to the tropics.

DRINKS
I like to embrace a theme wholeheartedly, so since the food is smoky and special, a Pouilly Fumé would make a splendid fragrant accompaniment to this feast.

PLANNING NOTES
The sauce for the plantains can be prepared eight hours in advance, then reheated. Soak the chicken livers for two hours before you cook them. Grill the tuna first, serving it with a garnish of parsley and chervil, before barbecuing the livers.
See pages 148–49 for recipes.

and air

VEGETARIAN SPECIAL
❧

The rich earthy taste of mushrooms, tangy roasted goat cheese, and seared polenta; every mouthful is ambrosia. *Serves 6*

SEARED GOAT CHEESE & TAPENADE
These two strong ingredients complement each other, particularly when served on fragrant, herby focaccia.

MIXED MUSHROOM KEBABS
Mushrooms, artichokes, and shallots are roasted over charcoal for a richly flavored trio.

PUMPKIN POLENTA
A northern Italian staple, enhanced with pumpkin and herbs, then seared on the grill.

DRINKS
A good Loire Sancerre or a New Zealand Sauvignon would suit the intense flavors of this repast.

PLANNING NOTES
Tapenade will keep for one week when stored in an airtight container. Make the mushroom marinade up to two days in advance, but do not marinate them for longer than 18 hours. Prepare the polenta to the end of step 4 the day before, to allow it to set. Its sauce can be made up to eight hours in advance, but do not add the cooked broccoli until the end. *See pages 150–51 for recipes.*

FEAST FOR A CROWD
❧

These deliciously tender marinated dishes are simple to prepare for large numbers of guests. *Serves 12*

GINGER & GARLIC CHICKEN
Well marinated, the chicken becomes mouthwateringly tender.

SEARED BEEF WITH THAI SAUCE
Do not be tempted to make this dish any spicier, or it will detract from the flavor of the meat.

AROMATIC RICE SALAD
Tender rice, fragrant with spices and herbs.

DRINKS
Lightly warmed sake, lager, and iced tea are the best refreshments for such spicy food.

PLANNING NOTES
Prepare the rice salad and the marinades for the chicken and the beef up to 12 hours in advance. Place the beef in to marinate immediately, but marinate the chicken for only up to six hours. The beef takes twice as long to cook as the chicken, so start cooking it 15 minutes before the chicken. *See pages 152–53 for recipes.*

SEAFOOD GRILL FOR 12

CHARRED SQUID

🥄 15 MINUTES   🍲 4 MINUTES   🍶 4 HOURS MARINATING

INGREDIENTS
6 TBSP (90ML) OLIVE OIL
3 TBSP RED WINE VINEGAR
2 KIWI FRUITS, JUICE & PULP
4 GARLIC CLOVES, FINELY CHOPPED
4 SPRIGS FRESH ROSEMARY
12 SPRIGS FRESH MARJORAM
12 SQUID, PREPARED FOR COOKING
1 CUP (125G) ALL-PURPOSE FLOUR
1 TBSP DRIED MARJORAM

COOK'S TIP
Be very careful not to overcook the squid; it quickly becomes tough.

1 To make the marinade, place the oil, vinegar, juice and pulp of the kiwi fruits, garlic, and herb sprigs in a nonmetallic bowl.

2 Rinse the squid, dry well, and slice the body into 3 pieces lengthwise.

3 Add the squid (body and small tentacles) to the marinade. Cover, and let marinate in the refrigerator for at least 4 hours.

4 Remove the squid, wiping off and reserving as much of the marinade as possible. Dip each piece into the flour and dried marjoram.

5 Baste the squid with the marinade and grill on the barbecue for about 2 minutes on each side, until browned. Serve immediately.

CHARRED SQUID

NEW POTATO SALAD

RED MULLET WITH FENNEL & ORANGE

146

RED MULLET WITH FENNEL & ORANGE

30 MINUTES · 10 MINUTES

INGREDIENTS
1 LARGE WHOLE EGG (IF USING BLENDER)
OR 2 EGG YOLKS (IF WHISKING BY HAND)
2½ TSP DIJON MUSTARD
SALT & PEPPER TO TASTE
1 LEMON, JUICE ONLY
⅔ CUP (150ML) VEGETABLE OIL
⅔ CUP (150ML) OLIVE OIL,
PLUS 3 TBSP FOR BASTING
1 ORANGE, JUICE & GRATED ZEST
1 TBSP FENNEL SEEDS, GROUND
6 RED MULLET, FILLETED
NEW POTATO SALAD (SEE PAGE 186)
AND SALAD GREENS TO SERVE

1 To make the mayonnaise, beat the whole egg or egg yolks, ½ teaspoon of mustard, and salt to taste until thickened. Stir in 1 tablespoon of lemon juice. Add a few drops of the vegetable oil, stir well, and then add the remaining amount in a slow, steady stream, beating constantly.

2 When all the vegetable oil has been incorporated and the mixture has started to thicken, add the ⅔ cup (150ml) of olive oil very slowly, beating constantly until the mayonnaise is very thick. Season to taste.

3 Stir in the zest of the orange and half the juice. Cover with plastic wrap and refrigerate until needed.

4 In a small bowl, combine the rest of the orange juice, the fennel, the remaining mustard and 3 tablespoons of olive oil. Baste the fish fillets with this mixture.

5 Grill the fillets for 3 minutes on each side until the skin is golden and the flesh is no longer opaque. Serve with a dollop of mayonnaise, New Potato Salad, and salad greens.

COOK'S TIPS
Dried or fresh fennel stalks placed on the coals during grilling impart a wonderful flavor to the red mullet. Bay leaves (or leafy twigs) could also be used. The mayonnaise can be prepared in advance; it keeps in the refrigerator for 1 week.

PEPPERED PINEAPPLE

15 MINUTES · 12 MINUTES

INGREDIENTS
2 PINEAPPLES
4 TBSP UNSALTED BUTTER
1 LEMON, JUICE ONLY
1 TBSP GROUND BLACK PEPPER
1 CUP (250ML) PINEAPPLE JUICE
1 LIME, JUICE ONLY
2 TSP ORANGE FLOWER WATER

1 Cut the top and bottom off the pineapples and peel. Cut each pineapple into 6 wedges. Remove the tough central cores, and cut grooves along the width to remove the eyes.

2 Rub butter and lemon juice all over the pineapple wedges and sprinkle with coarse pepper.

3 To make the sauce, heat the pineapple and lime juices in a saucepan and boil until reduced by half. Stir in the orange flower water.

4 Grill the pineapple for about 6 minutes on each side, until golden. Pour over the fruit juices and serve.

COOK'S TIP
Increase or decrease the number of slices of pineapple according to the size of your party. Increase the sauce proportionately, but do not reduce it by more than half.

GOURMET BARBECUE FOR 6

TEA-SMOKED TUNA

✓ 10 Minutes 🍲 10 Minutes

INGREDIENTS
2½ LB (1.25KG) TUNA, IN 6 X ½ IN (1CM) STEAKS
SALT & PEPPER TO TASTE
4 TBSP OLIVE OIL
2 TBSP EACH LAPSANG SOUCHONG TEA LEAVES
& GREEN OR CHINA TEA LEAVES
4 TBSP SOFT BROWN SUGAR
MARJORAM SPRIGS TO GARNISH

1 Brush the tuna steaks with oil and season to taste. Set aside.

2 Line a large wok with foil. Combine the teas and sugar and place inside the wok on the foil.

3 When the barbecue is very hot, cover the wok and place over the flame. When the tea mixture begins to smoke, place a wire rack inside the wok, and lay as many slices of tuna on the rack as it will hold.

4 Cook for about 5 minutes, turning halfway through cooking, until the tuna is pale brown on the outside but still pink in the middle, then remove and keep warm. Repeat with the remaining tuna, using the same tea mixture. Garnish with marjoram sprigs and serve with salad greens.

COOK'S TIP
Be careful not to oversmoke the tuna, as you risk overwhelming the flavor of the fish.

CRISPY CHICKEN LIVERS

✓ 10 Minutes 🍲 10 Minutes ⏲ 2 Hours Soaking

INGREDIENTS
1½ LB (750G) CHICKEN LIVERS
⅔ CUP (150ML) MILK
2 TBSP WHITE VINEGAR
2 CUPS (100G) FRESH WHITE BREAD CRUMBS
1 TBSP FRESH THYME, FINELY CHOPPED
SALT & PEPPER TO TASTE
6 TBSP (90ML) DIJON MUSTARD
4 TBSP OLIVE OIL
SALAD GREENS TO SERVE

1 Rinse the chicken livers and remove any white sinew. Place the livers in a bowl and cover with the milk and vinegar. Let soak at least 2 hours.

2 Just before cooking, drain the livers and pat dry with paper towels. Discard the milk and vinegar.

3 Combine the bread crumbs, thyme, and seasoning. Coat the livers in the mustard, roll them in the bread crumb mixture, and dab with oil.

4 Place the chicken livers on a greased wire rack on the grill and cook for about 5 minutes on each side, dabbing with extra oil if necessary, until they are crispy on the outside and slightly pink inside. Serve immediately on a bed of salad greens.

COOK'S TIP
For the best results, cook these on the grill while the coals are still hot. Place the livers at medium height above the coals.

ROASTED PLANTAINS WITH RUM SAUCE

10 MINUTES ✎ 7 MINUTES 🍲

INGREDIENTS
6 RIPE (ALMOST BLACK) SWEET PLANTAINS
3 LIMES, JUICE ONLY
2 TBSP DARK RUM
4 TBSP UNSALTED BUTTER
4 TBSP SOFT BROWN SUGAR
LIGHT CREAM OR ICE CREAM TO SERVE

1 Cut the plantains in half lengthwise. Brush the cut side with the juice of 1 lime, and roast on the grill, skin side down, for 3 minutes.

2 While the plantains are cooking, heat the rum, half the butter, the remaining lime juice, and the sugar in a small saucepan, until the sugar has dissolved. Remove from the heat.

3 Brush the cut sides of the plantains with the remaining butter and turn over, cut side to the flame. Roast for 3–4 minutes more, until dark golden. Pour the sauce over the plantains and serve with light cream or ice cream.

COOK'S TIPS
If plantains are unavailable, large bananas are also delicious cooked in this way. The sauce can be made a day in advance and reheated.

ROASTED PLANTAINS WITH
RUM SAUCE

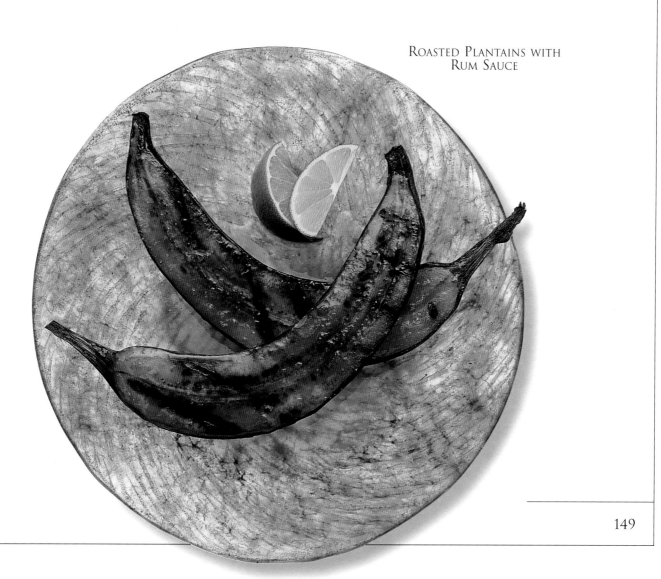

VEGETARIAN SPECIAL FOR 6

SEARED GOAT CHEESE & TAPENADE

⏱ 10 MINUTES 🍲 4 MINUTES

INGREDIENTS
½ LB (250G) BLACK OLIVES, PITTED
2OZ (60G) CAPERS
5 FRESH SAGE LEAVES
2 GARLIC CLOVES, COARSELY CHOPPED
6 TBSP (90ML) OLIVE OIL
2 TSP BALSAMIC VINEGAR
½ LEMON, JUICE & GRATED ZEST
6 SMALL GOAT CHEESES
SALAD GREENS, Walnut Dressing
(SEE PAGE 185) & FOCACCIA (SEE PAGE 186)
TO SERVE

1 To make the tapenade, blend together all the ingredients (except the cheese) in a food processor to a smooth but slightly grainy paste.

2 Divide the cheeses horizontally in half and grill skin side down for 2 minutes, until they just begin to melt.

3 Serve the seared goat cheese on a bed of salad greens with Walnut Dressing, a spoonful of tapenade, and Focaccia. Break the bread into chunks, and sear over the grill for about 2 minutes on each side before serving.

COOK'S TIP
Watch the cheese carefully while grilling; do not allow it to melt and drip over the coals.

SEARED GOAT
CHEESE

FOCACCIA

TAPENADE

150

MIXED MUSHROOM KEBABS

55 MINUTES   35 MINUTES   2 HOURS MARINATING

INGREDIENTS

4 SHALLOTS, FINELY CHOPPED, PLUS 24 WHOLE
SHALLOTS, UNPEELED
2 TBSP FRESH SAGE, FINELY CHOPPED, PLUS 12
WHOLE SAGE LEAVES
3 GARLIC CLOVES, CRUSHED
½ CUP (125ML) OLIVE OIL, PLUS
EXTRA FOR BASTING
1¼ LB (625G) MIXED MUSHROOMS
13OZ (400G) CANNED ARTICHOKE HEARTS,
HALVED
12 WOODEN BARBECUE SKEWERS
PUMPKIN POLENTA (SEE BELOW) TO SERVE

1 To make the marinade, place the chopped shallots, chopped sage, garlic, and olive oil in a nonmetallic bowl. Prepare the mushrooms (see Step 1, page 96) and add to the marinade. Stir gently. Cover and let marinate in the refrigerator for 2–18 hours, turning occasionally.

2 Soak the wooden skewers in water for 30 minutes. Meanwhile, grill the whole shallots on the barbecue for 30 minutes, until just cooked, then peel.

3 Thread the mushrooms and shallots onto the skewers with the whole sage leaves and artichokes. Dab with a little oil and grill for 5 minutes per side, basting with the oil occasionally during cooking, until golden and tender. Serve with a green salad and Pumpkin Polenta.

PUMPKIN POLENTA

35 MINUTES   1 HOUR 15 MINUTES   12 HOURS SETTING

INGREDIENTS

½ CUP (125ML) OLIVE OIL
5 GARLIC CLOVES, FINELY CHOPPED
¾ LB (375G) PUMPKIN, PEELED AND COARSELY
CHOPPED
SALT & PEPPER TO TASTE
6 CUPS (1.5 LITERS) WATER
2 TSP SALT
¾ LB (375G) PRECOOKED INSTANT POLENTA
3½ TBSP FRESH OREGANO, FINELY CHOPPED
1½ TSP GROUND BLACK PEPPER
½ CUP (125G) BUTTER
2 ONIONS, FINELY CHOPPED
1LB (500G) TOMATOES, PEELED & CHOPPED
1 TBSP TOMATO PASTE
1 CUP (250ML) VEGETABLE STOCK
(SEE PAGE 185)
¾ LB (375G) BROCCOLI, CUT INTO SMALL
FLORETS & TENDER STEMS DICED
3OZ (90G) PARMESAN CHEESE, GRATED

1 Heat 2 tablespoons of the oil in a saucepan, add 2 garlic cloves and the pumpkin, and sauté gently for 5 minutes, until dark golden. Cover the pumpkin with lightly salted water, and simmer, covered, for 20 minutes. Drain and mash half of the pumpkin. Reserve the rest for the sauce.

2 To make the polenta, fill a large saucepan with 6 cups (1.5 liters) water, add the 2 teaspoons of salt, and bring to a boil. Put the polenta into a pitcher and pour it into the pan in a steady stream, beating constantly to prevent lumps from forming.

3 Add 1½ tablespoons of oregano and pepper, then turn down the heat to the lowest setting. Cook for 10 minutes, stirring constantly, until the spoon can stand up in the mixture. As soon as the polenta is ready, stir in the mashed pumpkin and butter.

4 Spoon the polenta into a greased 12in (30cm) square pan and leave, covered, overnight to set.

5 For the sauce, heat 2 tablespoons of the oil in a saucepan and gently sauté the onions and remaining garlic for about 10 minutes, stirring, until pale golden and softened.

6 Add the tomatoes, tomato paste, remaining oregano, and stock. Season and cook for about 10 minutes, until the sauce has reduced to a liquid pulp. Stir in the broccoli and remaining pumpkin pieces, cover, and cook for 4 minutes, until the broccoli is *al dente*.

7 Cut the set polenta into 24 slices, brush with the remaining olive oil, and grill for about 8 minutes on each side, until golden. Sprinkle with the Parmesan and serve hot with the sauce and the Mixed Mushroom Kebabs.

FEAST FOR A CROWD FOR 12

GINGER & GARLIC CHICKEN

10 Minutes   25 Minutes   2 Hours Marinating

INGREDIENTS
4 cups (1 liter) plain yogurt
5 limes (juice & grated zest of 3, plus 2 cut into wedges to garnish)
3in (7cm) piece of fresh ginger, peeled & cut into thirds
1 tbsp each ground cumin, fenugreek & ground turmeric
3 garlic cloves, crushed
1 fresh red chili, seeded & finely chopped
3 shallots, finely chopped
12 chicken breasts, about 4lb (2kg), boned & skinned
Aromatic Rice Salad (see opposite) to serve

1 To make the marinade, blend all the ingredients (except the chicken, lime wedges, and rice salad), together in a food processor, until smooth.

2 Place the chicken breasts in a single layer in a large nonmetallic dish and prick lightly all over with a fork.

Spoon the marinade over the chicken. Cover and let marinate in the refrigerator for 2–6 hours.

3 Remove the chicken and shake off as much marinade as possible, reserving ⅔ cup (150ml) for the Aromatic Rice Salad (see opposite). Grill for about 8 minutes each side, until it is golden and tender. Garnish with lime wedges and serve with Aromatic Rice Salad and a red-leaf salad.

AROMATIC RICE SALAD

GINGER & GARLIC CHICKEN

152

SEARED BEEF WITH THAI SAUCE

25 MINUTES   30 MINUTES   4 HOURS MARINATING

INGREDIENTS
7 GARLIC CLOVES, CRUSHED
7 FRESH RED CHILIES, SEEDED
& FINELY CHOPPED
5 LIMES, JUICE & GRATED ZEST
3LB (1.5KG) BEEF SIRLOIN
½ CUP (125ML) WATER
5 TBSP (75ML) WHITE VINEGAR
6 ANCHOVY FILLETS, MASHED
2 SHALLOTS, FINELY CHOPPED
2½ TBSP FISH SAUCE
1 TBSP SUPERFINE SUGAR
AROMATIC RICE SALAD (SEE BELOW) TO SERVE

1 To make the marinade, mix together 4 garlic cloves, 4 chilies, and the juice and zest of 3 limes.

2 Place the beef in a nonmetallic dish and add the marinade. Cover and let marinate in the refrigerator for about 4 hours, turning the beef over halfway through.

3 To make the sauce, combine the water, vinegar, anchovies, shallots, fish sauce, superfine sugar, and the remaining garlic, chilies, and lime juice and zest. Cover with plastic wrap and refrigerate until needed.

4 Remove the beef from the refrigerator and shake off as much marinade as possible. Transfer to the barbecue and grill for about 15 minutes on each side, basting with the marinade halfway through cooking, until the meat is golden on the outside but still pink in the middle.

5 Let the beef rest in a warm place for 5 minutes, then carve it into thin slices. Pour over the sauce. Serve with the Aromatic Rice Salad.

AROMATIC RICE SALAD

10 MINUTES   15 MINUTES   30 MINUTES SOAKING

INGREDIENTS
5 CUPS (1KG) BASMATI RICE
4 TBSP PEANUT OIL
2 TBSP BUTTER
20 CARDAMOM PODS, CRUSHED
3 CUPS (750ML) WATER
⅔ CUP (150ML) RESERVED MARINADE (SEE
STEP 3 OPPOSITE)
1 ORANGE PEPPER, SEEDED & CUT INTO
SMALL, THIN STRIPS
3 TSP SALT
GINGER & GARLIC CHICKEN (SEE OPPOSITE)
TO SERVE

1 Wash the rice in a sieve under running water until the water runs clear. Soak for 30 minutes, then drain thoroughly for 5 minutes.

2 Heat the oil and butter in a large saucepan over moderate heat until the butter just begins to brown. Immediately add the rice and the cardamom pods, stirring until they are well coated. Cook for about 2 minutes, then add the water, marinade, pepper slices, and salt.

3 Bring to a boil, turn the heat down to very low, and cover. Cook for 9 minutes, then remove from the heat, stir, fluff up with a fork, and let cool in the covered pan. Serve hot or cold, with Ginger and Garlic Chicken and a mixed salad.

PICNICS

INVITE YOUR FRIENDS TO JOIN YOU FOR A PICNIC IN THE COUNTRYSIDE OR BY THE SEA. UNPACK THE HAMPERS, AND SAVOR THE LUXURIOUS LANGUOR OF A PROTRACTED OUTDOOR MEAL. COMBINE SIMPLE BUT SPECIAL FLAVORS OF GOOD FOOD WITH CHILLED WHITE WINE, BEER, OR FRESH FRUIT JUICE. PICNICS ARE A WONDERFUL WAY TO CREATE A SMALL PATCH OF PARADISE, LEAVING A FEELING OF RELAXATION AND RENEWAL, A SENSE OF HAVING TAKEN A VACATION.

Once you and your guests are replete with Herbed Country Pâté and Parslied Ham from the Country Hamper menu (page 158), lie back and enjoy the sky (right).

SUMMER

Lazy, hazy summer days of meals, to the

ONE OF THE BEST aspects of picnics is that the work is done in advance, leaving you free to concentrate on setting up, serving, and enjoying the occasion itself.

PACKING FOR A PICNIC

Wrap plates and cutlery in decorative cotton napkins and tea towels, and transport in large wicker baskets. Pack the food and drinks in cake tins and cooler bags.

1 Fold a cotton napkin in half. Place a set of cutlery pointing from top left toward the middle, and start to wrap the napkin loosely around it.

2 Roll the napkin in a slight semicircle to form a cone. Secure it about two-thirds of the way down by tying several strands of raffia firmly around the cutlery in a bow.

3 Arrange the napkin rolls in a box in a basket with other nonfood items, packed firmly to prevent breakage. Use the picnic cloth to protect fragile items, or to shield the food from direct sunlight.

YELLOW & BLUE
Keep to an informal color scheme, and don't worry if items don't match exactly.

TABLECLOTH
If you are picnicking on the ground, spread a small cloth on a larger undercloth to keep the food well clear of sand or dirt.

sound of waves or rustling leaves

SEASHELLS
Decorate your picnic table with elements from the surrounding area: a plate of shells, for example, for a seaside picnic.

CUTLERY BASKET
A square box, centrally placed for accessibility, holds the wrapped cutlery for each guest. Use the box to keep it together after the meal.

HERB BUNCHES
Make small bunches of herbs for all your guests. They can take them home after the picnic and hang them up to dry out.

MENUS

To eat under the skies is bliss

COUNTRY HAMPER

No one will go hungry after sampling soda bread,
ham cooked with parsley, and a coarse herby pâté.
Serves 12

RAISIN & OREGANO SODA BREAD
*Quick and easy to make, it is almost impossible to resist
eating this bread as it comes out of the oven.*

PARSLIED HAM
*Ham and vegetables set in a tangy stock make a traditional
Easter dish in France.*

HERBED COUNTRY PÂTÉ
*Made from pork and chicken, this pâté looks and tastes
wonderfully rich.*

DRINKS
*Choose a Bourgogne Aligote, served chilled, to partner
this picnic. If you would prefer a red wine, Merlot is a
good alternative.*

PLANNING NOTES
The parslied ham improves with time; ideally, prepare it
three days in advance, but at least a day before eating. Both
the ham and the pâté will keep for one week, covered, in the
refrigerator. The bread is best when freshly made, but can be
frozen for up to six weeks. *See pages 160–61 for recipes.*

FRENCH PICNIC

Two dishes from the south of France, and an
upside-down tart, make this an appealing menu
for a late summer picnic. *Serves 6*

PISSALADIÈRE
Enjoy this French "pizza" hot or cold.

SALAD NIÇOISE
A hearty salad packed with the flavors of the sun.

QUINCE TART TATIN
*Quince are wonderfully perfumed, but both apples and pears
are good alternatives in this upside-down tart.*

DRINKS
*As the picnic has a French flavor, choose French wine –
a white Bordeaux or a good rosé from the south.*

PLANNING NOTES
Enjoy the pissaladière fresh, up to 24 hours after it is made,
or freeze it for a maximum of six weeks; it is delicious hot or
cold. The salad must be prepared on the day of the picnic,
and dressed at the last moment. The tart is best eaten within
a day of being made. *See pages 162–63 for recipes.*

EXOTIC SPREAD

Asian food may not be the first thing that comes to mind for a picnic, but this spicy feast is well worth trying. *Serves 12*

SPICY CHICKEN WITH PAPAYA SALAD
Ginger and garlic are predominant flavors in this dish, balanced by the wonderfully fresh-tasting papaya salad.

SPICY LAMB KEBABS
Skewered pieces of lamb are meltingly tender, with a sweet and sour chili and cumin sauce.

INDIAN MILK PUDDING
This creamy rice pudding with a burnt-sugar topping slices easily. Perfect for a picnic.

DRINKS
Cold beer, preferably Indian Kingfisher Lager, is the best alcohol to accompany these tangy dishes. Chilled sparkling water with slices of lime is also refreshing.

PLANNING NOTES
The milk pudding will keep for four to five days in the refrigerator, but it is best to grill the sugar topping the morning before eating. Both the meat dishes improve with time, and can be kept for one or two days in the refrigerator. *See pages 164–65 for recipes.*

DINE IN STYLE

These dishes are ideal for an elegant picnic, perhaps for an outdoor concert, the races, or for a celebratory meal somewhere special. *Serves 6*

DUCK & ARUGULA SALAD
Duck, marinated in sherry vinegar and cooked with olives and rosemary, is served thinly sliced on a bed of arugula.

FENNEL & CHEESE TART
These two flavors complement each other so well; combine them in an easy-to-eat tart.

POLENTA CAKE
Serve small slices of this rich-textured cake – that way there will be plenty left for second helpings later in the day.

DRINKS
Full-bodied California Zinfandel or Italian Amarone della Valpollicella would suit both the duck and the tart. Follow with a moderately sweet Vin Santo from Tuscany to enjoy with the polenta cake.

PLANNING NOTES
All three dishes can be made 24 hours in advance, although the salad should be assembled at the last minute. Refrigerate the duck in an airtight container, either whole or cut into slices to keep it from drying out. Store the cake upside down in a cake tin so its base sits on the lid; this makes it easy to cut without transferring it to a plate. *See pages 166–67 for recipes.*

COUNTRY HAMPER FOR 12

RAISIN & OREGANO SODA BREAD

15 MINUTES · 40 MINUTES

INGREDIENTS
2¼ CUPS (300G) WHOLE-WHEAT FLOUR
2¼ CUPS (300G) ALL-PURPOSE FLOUR
1 TSP BAKING SODA
2 TSP BAKING POWDER
2 TBSP SUGAR
1 TSP SALT
1 LARGE EGG
6 TBSP (90ML) MILK
½ CUP (350ML) PLAIN YOGURT
½ CUP (125G) RAISINS
2 TSP FRESH OREGANO, FINELY CHOPPED

COOK'S TIP
To test if the bread is done, tap the bottom of the loaf with your knuckles. If it sounds hollow, the bread is ready.

1 Preheat oven to 375°F/190°C. In a large mixing bowl, sift both types of flour, the baking soda, baking powder, sugar, and salt.

2 Lightly beat the egg, milk, and yogurt, and add to the mixing bowl, together with the raisins and oregano.

3 With your hand, draw the flour into the yogurt mixture to make a soft, sticky dough. On a floured work surface, knead the dough for about 2 minutes, then shape it into a round loaf about 2in (5cm) high.

4 With floured hands, transfer the loaf to a lined baking sheet, cut a cross ¼in (5mm) deep in the center, and bake for 40 minutes, until the bread is brown. Remove from the oven, and transfer to a wire rack to cool.

CELERIAC RÉMOULADE

HERBED COUNTRY PÂTÉ

PARSLIED HAM

PARSLIED HAM

☑ 25 MINUTES 🍲 2 HOURS 50 MINUTES ☐ 24 HOURS SOAKING PLUS 12 HOURS CHILLING

INGREDIENTS

5LB (2.5KG) UNCOOKED HAM,
SOAKED FOR 24 HOURS
3 CUPS (750ML) DRY WHITE WINE
12 SHALLOTS, PEELED & HALVED
6 CARROTS, CUT INTO LARGE ROUNDS
2 CELERY STICKS, CUT INTO LARGE SLICES
2 GARLIC CLOVES, PEELED & HALVED
3 BAY LEAVES
2 SPRIGS EACH FRESH ROSEMARY & TARRAGON
4 SPRIGS FRESH SAGE
6 SPRIGS FRESH THYME
1 TBSP GREEN PEPPERCORNS
2½ TBSP POWDERED GELATIN
6 TBSP (90ML) WATER
5 TBSP (75 ML) TARRAGON OR WHITE VINEGAR
6 TBSP (90ML) BRANDY (OPTIONAL)
2 BUNCHES FRESH FLAT-LEAF PARSLEY, FINELY
CHOPPED, PLUS 12 SPRIGS TO GARNISH
CELERIAC RÉMOULADE (SEE PAGE 187) TO SERVE

1 Rinse the soaked ham and place it in a large saucepan with the wine, shallots, carrots, celery, garlic, bay leaves, rosemary, tarragon, sage, thyme, and peppercorns. Pour over enough water to cover the ham, bring to a boil, and simmer for 2½ hours, until well done. Let cool.

2 Remove the ham and strain the stock, reserving the vegetables. Bring the stock to the boil, and reduce to 4 cups (1 liter).

3 Meanwhile, sprinkle the gelatin onto the water in a small saucepan. Let soak for 5 minutes. Warm over a very low heat until the gelatin has dissolved and the liquid is clear. Add the vinegar and brandy, if using, to the simmering stock, then whisk in the gelatin. Taste and adjust seasoning. Let the stock cool for 2–3 hours, until it nears setting point.

4 While the stock is cooling, trim off skin and fat and cut the meat into both large and small chunks. In alternating layers, arrange the meat, vegetables, and chopped parsley in an 8 cup (2 liter) deep oval bowl or terrine. Add the stock just before it sets. Cover with plastic wrap and refrigerate for at least 12 hours. Garnish with parsley and serve with Celeriac Rémoulade.

COOK'S TIPS
This is best made 3 days in advance. Carry to the picnic in a cooler and serve from the bowl.

HERBED COUNTRY PÂTÉ

☑ 20 MINUTES 🍲 2 HOURS 15 MINUTES ☐ 24 HOURS MARINATING

INGREDIENTS

6 TBSP (90ML) MEDIUM SHERRY
6 TBSP (90ML) BRANDY
3 GARLIC CLOVES, CRUSHED
3 BAY LEAVES, PLUS 6 TO GARNISH
1 TBSP FRESH TARRAGON, FINELY CHOPPED
1 TSP SALT
½ TSP GROUND WHITE PEPPER
1¼ LB (625G) CHICKEN LIVERS, CUT INTO
½ IN (1CM) CUBES
¾ LB (375G) PORK BELLY, TRIMMED, CUT INTO
½ IN (1CM) CUBES
½ LB (250G) GROUND PORK
½ LB (250G) SMOKED BACON
3 CHICKEN BREASTS, BONED & SKINNED, CUT
INTO 2 X ¾ IN (5 X 2CM) STRIPS
6 PICKLED GHERKINS, QUARTERED LENGTHWISE

1 To make the marinade, combine the sherry, brandy, garlic, 3 bay leaves, tarragon, and seasoning in a large, nonmetallic bowl.

2 Add the chicken livers, pork belly, and ground pork. Cover and let marinate in the refrigerator for 24 hours, turning occasionally. Discard the bay leaves.

3 Preheat oven to 400°F/200°C. Grease a 9 x 5in (23 x 12cm) terrine or loaf pan. Line the bottom and sides with bacon strips, stretching them over the back of a knife if necessary. Leave them hanging over the edge of the terrine. Set the remaining bacon aside.

4 In the terrine, place one-third of the marinated meat, followed by one-third of the marinade, then the chicken. Repeat, adding the gherkins instead of the chicken. Finally, spoon over the remaining meat and marinade.

5 Fold over the bacon, lay the reserved slices on top, and decorate the surface with 6 bay leaves. Cover with foil. Place the terrine in a roasting pan filled with boiling water and cook for 2¼ hours. Serve cold with Raisin & Oregano Soda Bread (see opposite).

COOK'S TIPS
This pâté is best made a few days in advance. It will keep for 1 week in the refrigerator.

FRENCH PICNIC FOR 6

PISSALADIÈRE

🥄 30 MINUTES 🍲 45 MINUTES

INGREDIENTS

¾ LB (375G) PUFF PASTRY (SEE PAGE 184)
2 TBSP OLIVE OIL
6 MEDIUM ONIONS, THINLY SLICED
4 GARLIC CLOVES, CRUSHED
ABOUT 12 LARGE FRESH PLUM TOMATOES,
PEELED, SEEDED & COARSELY CHOPPED
2 TBSP TOMATO PASTE
2 TSP SUGAR
2 TBSP FRESH MARJORAM, FINELY CHOPPED,
PLUS 10 SPRIGS TO GARNISH
10 ANCHOVY FILLETS, HALVED LENGTHWISE
SALT & PEPPER TO TASTE
1 EGG, YOLK ONLY
1 TSP MILK
30 BLACK OLIVES, PITTED

1 For the crust, roll out the pastry into a 13in (32cm) circle, then cut a 1in (2.5cm) strip from around the outside. Brush the strip with water and lay it over the edge of the 12in (30cm) circle to form a rim made from a double layer of pastry.

2 Make a crisscross pattern around the rim with a knife. Prick the bottom of the tart all over with a fork. Refrigerate for 30 minutes.

3 Meanwhile, prepare the filling. Preheat oven to 400°F/200°C. Heat the olive oil in a saucepan and cook the onions and garlic, covered, for about 18 minutes, stirring from time to time, until softened. Add the tomatoes, tomato paste, sugar, and chopped marjoram and cook for about 5 minutes over medium heat, stirring occasionally, to make a thick purée.

4 Spread the onion mixture over the pastry shell. Arrange the marjoram sprigs and anchovies on top, radiating out from the center. Sprinkle with salt and pepper, and brush the edge of the tart with the egg yolk mixed with milk.

5 Bake for 20–25 minutes, until the pastry has puffed around the edges. Remove from the oven and decorate with the olives.

PISSALADIÈRE

SALAD NIÇOISE

20 MINUTES · 25 MINUTES

INGREDIENTS

24 BABY NEW POTATOES, ABOUT
1LB (500G), SCRUBBED
½LB (250G) THIN GREEN BEANS
5OZ (150G) FRESH PEAS, SHELLED
3 EGGS
1LB (500G) FRESH OR CANNED TUNA
12 ANCHOVY FILLETS
6 TOMATOES, CUT INTO WEDGES
¼ CUP (100G) BLACK OLIVES, UNPITTED
6 SCALLIONS, THINLY SLICED LENGTHWISE
HALF A CUCUMBER, THINLY SLICED
1 FENNEL BULB, THINLY SLICED
18 RADISHES
SALAD GREENS
2 TSP EACH OF FRESH HERBS, FINELY CHOPPED:
THYME, OREGANO, MARJORAM, MINT
3 TBSP FRESH BASIL, SHREDDED
¾ CUP (175ML) VINAIGRETTE (SEE PAGE 185)

1 In a saucepan of salted boiling water, cook the potatoes for about 15 minutes, or until soft. When cool, slice them in half. Cook the beans and peas in boiling water for 2–3 minutes. Refresh under cold water and drain.

2 Cook the eggs in simmering water for 9 minutes, until the yolk is just set. Rinse under cold water. Peel and slice them into quarters.

3 If you are using fresh tuna, preheat the broiler to moderate. Cut the tuna into slices ½in (1cm) thick, brush with olive oil, and grill for 2 minutes on each side, until just cooked. Remove from broiler and flake. If using canned tuna, drain well then flake.

4 Arrange all the ingredients in a large bowl. Just before eating, pour over the Vinaigrette, toss, and serve with freshly sliced French bread.

COOK'S TIP
It is best to cut the eggs and add them to the salad just before serving.

QUINCE TART TATIN

10 MINUTES · 1 HOUR 55 MINUTES

INGREDIENTS

½ CUP (125G) UNSALTED BUTTER
½ CUP (125G) SUGAR
2LB (1KG) QUINCES, PEELED
OR PEARS, UNPEELED
3 TBSP BRANDY (OPTIONAL)
10OZ (300G) SWEET SHORTCRUST PASTRY,
CHILLED (SEE PAGE 184)
1 TBSP CONFECTIONERS' SUGAR, SIFTED
2 CUPS (500ML) HEAVY CREAM
2 TBSP BRANDY OR OTHER LIQUEUR

COOK'S TIP
If you are using the pastry recipe on page 184, make 1½ times the quantities given, or double the recipe and freeze the excess.

1 Heat the butter and sugar in a 9in (23cm) all-metal skillet over moderate heat until the mixture begins to caramelize. Remove from the heat.

2 Cut the quinces into quarters, remove the cores, and cut each quarter into 3 slices (if using pears, cut into quarters).

3 Arrange the fruit, core side up, in a radiating pattern in the pan. Cook over low heat for 1½ hours (40 minutes for pears), until soft, shaking the pan occasionally. Heat the brandy in a small pan or ladle, then set it alight and carefully pour it over the fruit.

4 Preheat oven to 375°F/190°C. Roll out the pastry into a circle just a little larger than the pan. Lay it over the pan, tucking the edges down into the pan to cover the fruit. Bake for 20 minutes, until pale golden. Remove and cool for 5–10 minutes.

5 Meanwhile, make the brandied cream. Place the confectioners' sugar, cream, and brandy in a large bowl and whisk until the mixture forms soft peaks. Put the tart tatin onto a flat serving platter; the pastry now forms the base, the fruit the top. Serve with the brandied cream.

EXOTIC SPREAD FOR 12

SPICY CHICKEN WITH PAPAYA SALAD

— ☑ 35 MINUTES ⌂ 50 MINUTES ☐ 2 HOURS SOAKING —

INGREDIENTS

3IN (7CM) PIECE OF FRESH GINGER,
PEELED & COARSELY CHOPPED
4 GARLIC CLOVES, PEELED
2 FRESH RED CHILIES, SEEDED &
COARSELY CHOPPED
SCANT 1 CUP (200ML) CANNED COCONUT MILK
4 TBSP OLIVE OIL
24 CHICKEN THIGHS, BONED, SKINS ON
2 TBSP GROUND CORIANDER
3 TBSP GROUND CUMIN
3 TBSP CARDAMOMS, SEEDS CRUSHED
½ A FRESH COCONUT, GRATED
& LIGHTLY TOASTED
3 LIMES, JUICE & GRATED ZEST
2 TBSP SUGAR
1¼ CUPS (300ML) WATER
5 TBSP (75G) FRESH
CILANTRO,
COARSELY
CHOPPED
⅔ CUP (150ML)
SHARP SWEET
DRESSING (SEE
PAGE 185)
4 LARGE RIPE
PAPAYAS, PEELED
& THINLY
SLICED
6 ZUCCHINIS,
CUT INTO THIN
STRIPS
1 CUCUMBER,
THINLY SLICED

1 In a blender, purée the ginger, garlic, chilies, and coconut milk to make a smooth paste.

2 Heat the oil in a large skillet and cook the chicken in batches for approximately 5 minutes on each side, until evenly browned. Remove from the skillet and set aside.

3 To the skillet, add the ground coriander, cumin, and cardamom seeds and cook over high heat for about 2 minutes. Stir in the spice paste and cook for 2 minutes more. Add the chicken, coconut, lime juice and zest, sugar, and water. Bring to a boil, cover, and simmer gently for 25 minutes. Add 2 tablespoons of the cilantro and let cool.

4 To make the salad, pour the Sharp Sweet Dressing over the papaya, zucchinis, and cucumber and let soak for at least 2 hours. Add the rest of the cilantro and serve with the chicken.

COOK'S TIPS

The chicken is also delicious served warm with the salad. If you wish, use mango instead of papaya.

SPICY CHICKEN WITH PAPAYA SALAD

SPICY LAMB KEBABS

20 MINUTES ☐ 12 MINUTES ☐ 2 HOURS MARINATING

INGREDIENTS

3 TBSP SESAME OIL
2 TBSP GROUND CUMIN
2 TBSP OYSTER SAUCE
3 TBSP SHERRY VINEGAR
2 TBSP LIGHT SOY SAUCE
3 TBSP DRY SHERRY
3 GARLIC CLOVES, CRUSHED
6 MILD FRESH GREEN CHILIES (PREFERABLY POBLANO OR ANCHO), FINELY CHOPPED
2 TBSP GROUND CUMIN
1 TBSP HONEY
3 LB (1.5 KG) BONED LEG OF LAMB, CUBED
2 KIWI FRUITS
24 METAL SKEWERS OR WOODEN SKEWERS, SOAKED FOR 1 HOUR

1 To make the marinade, heat the oil in a skillet. Add the cumin and lightly brown for about 2 minutes. Stir in all the remaining ingredients (except for the lamb and kiwi fruit), bring to a boil, then simmer for 5 minutes. Let cool.

2 Place the lamb in a large, nonmetallic bowl and squeeze over the kiwi juice and pulp. Add the marinade. Cover and let marinate in the refrigerator for 2–8 hours, turning occasionally.

3 Preheat the broiler to high. Line the bottom of the broiler pan with foil.

4 Remove the lamb from the bowl, reserving the marinade. Thread the meat onto the skewers.

5 Baste the lamb with the marinade and cook for about 6 minutes on each side, until crisp on the outside and just pink in the center. Let the kebabs cool.

COOK'S TIP
These kebabs may be prepared up to 3 days in advance and stored in the refrigerator.

INDIAN MILK PUDDING

10 MINUTES ☐ 25 MINUTES ☐ 12 HOURS CHILLING

INGREDIENTS

6 CUPS (1.5 LITERS) MILK
2 CUPS (500 G) ARBORIO RICE
3½ CUPS (850 ML) HEAVY CREAM
1 TSP GROUND SAFFRON
12 CARDAMOM PODS, SEEDS CRUSHED
1 TBSP GROUND CORIANDER
3 BAY LEAVES
1¾ CUPS (400 G) SUGAR
3 EGGS, LIGHTLY BEATEN
3 TSP VANILLA EXTRACT
1 TSP GROUND NUTMEG
CRÈME FRAÎCHE OR WHIPPED CREAM TO SERVE

1 In a large, heavy-bottomed saucepan, heat the milk, rice, cream, saffron, cardamom seeds, coriander, bay leaves, and half of the sugar. Bring to a boil, then simmer, covered, for about 20 minutes, until the rice is *al dente*. Remove from heat.

2 Discard the bay leaves. Beat in the eggs and vanilla until the mixture thickens. Pour into 2 rectangular 9 x 5in (23 x 13cm) loaf pans and let cool completely in a refrigerator, preferably overnight.

3 Turn the broiler to high. Sprinkle the remaining sugar mixed with the nutmeg over the tops of the desserts, and broil as close to the heat as possible for about 2–5 minutes, until the sugar caramelizes. When cold, cut into slices and serve with crème fraîche.

COOK'S TIP
Always broil the sugar topping as close to eating as possible. This pudding is also delicious served warm: after it has set overnight, heat it gently in a moderate oven for about 15 minutes, before broiling the topping.

DINE IN STYLE FOR 6

DUCK & ARUGULA SALAD

🗓 10 MINUTES 🍲 15 MINUTES 🗓 4 HOURS MARINATING

INGREDIENTS

4 DUCK BREASTS, SKINS LEFT ON

5 SPRIGS FRESH ROSEMARY

5 GARLIC CLOVES, SKINS LEFT ON, CRUSHED UNDER THE FLAT OF A KNIFE

⅔ CUP (150ML) SHERRY VINEGAR OR RED WINE VINEGAR

4 TBSP OLIVE OIL

SALT & PEPPER TO TASTE

24 BLACK OLIVES, PITTED & HALVED

ARUGULA LEAVES TO SERVE

PARMESAN CHEESE, THINLY SLICED, TO GARNISH

VINAIGRETTE (SEE PAGE 185)

COOK'S TIP

Use sherry vinegar instead of white vinegar when you make the Vinaigrette.

1 Flatten the duck breasts to 2in (5cm) thick. Make diagonal slits in the skin, and prick all over with a fork. Place the rosemary and garlic over the base of a nonmetallic dish and lay the duck in a single layer on top.

2 Combine the vinegar, 3 tablespoons of oil, and seasoning, and pour over the duck. Let marinate, covered, in the refrigerator for 4 hours; turn once.

3 Remove the duck and reserve the marinade. Heat the remaining oil in a large frying pan and brown the duck on both sides. Add the marinade, with the garlic and rosemary, and the olives. Cook over moderate heat for 5 minutes more on each side.

4 When the duck is cool enough to handle, remove the breasts and olives and wrap in plastic wrap to keep them moist. When completely cool, remove the plastic.

5 Cut the duck into slices ½ in (1cm) thick. Serve with the olives on a bed of arugula and garnish with Parmesan. Pour over the Vinaigrette.

DUCK & ARUGULA SALAD

FENNEL & CHEESE TART

25 MINUTES 50 MINUTES

INGREDIENTS

¾ LB (375G) SHORTCRUST PASTRY (SEE
PAGE 184)
4 EGGS: 1 YOLK ONLY, 3 WHOLE
2 TBSP BUTTER
1 TBSP VEGETABLE OIL
2 ONIONS, FINELY CHOPPED
1 GARLIC CLOVE, SKIN LEFT ON, CRUSHED
UNDER THE FLAT OF A KNIFE
2 FENNEL BULBS, CHOPPED
2 TSP FRESH THYME, FINELY CHOPPED
1¾ CUPS (450ML) PLAIN YOGURT
SALT TO TASTE
PINCH OF GROUND NUTMEG
4OZ (125G) GRUYÈRE CHEESE, GRATED
1 CUP (100G) WALNUTS, COARSELY CHOPPED,
PLUS WALNUT HALVES TO GARNISH
WALNUT DRESSING (SEE PAGE 185) TO SERVE

1 For the crust, roll out the pastry and press into a 10in (25cm) loose-bottomed, fluted tart pan. Prick the bottom of the pastry all over with a fork, then refrigerate for 30 minutes.

2 Preheat oven to 375°F/190°C. Line the dough with waxed paper, fill with dried beans, and bake in the oven for 12 minutes. Remove the waxed paper and the beans. Brush the bottom of the tart with the egg yolk, and return it to the oven to cook for 8 minutes more.

3 To make the filling, heat the butter and oil in a pan and gently sauté the onion, garlic, fennel, and thyme for 10 minutes, until soft. Discard the garlic.

4 In a large bowl, lightly beat the whole eggs, yogurt, salt, and nutmeg until just mixed. Stir in the Gruyère, chopped walnuts, and the onion and fennel mixture. Pour into the baked pastry shell and top with halved walnuts.

5 Bake for 30 minutes, until the top is golden. Serve cold with a green salad topped with walnuts and dressed with Walnut Dressing.

COOK'S TIPS

If you are using the pastry recipe on page 184, make 1½ times or double the quantities given and freeze the excess for up to 6 weeks. This tart will also make an excellent first course for a dinner or a delicious lunch.

POLENTA CAKE

25 MINUTES 1 HOUR

INGREDIENTS

1 CUP (250G) UNSALTED BUTTER, SOFTENED
1 CUP (200G) SUGAR
3 EGGS
½ CUP (75G) PINE NUTS, LIGHTLY TOASTED
¾ CUP (100G) RAISINS (PREFERABLY MUSCAT)
3 LEMONS: JUICE OF ½, GRATED ZEST OF 3
1 CUP (150G) POLENTA
1 TSP BAKING POWDER
10 CARDAMOM PODS, SEEDS CRUSHED
WHIPPED CREAM OR CRÈME FRAÎCHE TO SERVE

1 Preheat oven to 325°F/160°C. Cream the butter and sugar until pale and fluffy, then add the eggs, one by one, beating between each addition.

2 Fold in the pine nuts, raisins, and lemon juice and zest, then add the polenta, baking powder, and the cardamom pods. Mix well.

3 Pour the mixture into a greased and floured 8in (20cm) springform cake pan and bake for 1 hour.

4 Let the cake cool in its pan for 10 minutes, then release the sides. Let stand 20 minutes more, then transfer to a cake plate. Serve with a spoonful of whipped cream or crème fraîche.

COOK'S TIP

Try serving this cake warm as a lunch or dinner dessert; serve it with ⅔ cup (150ml) heavy cream, whipped with the juice of half a lemon and 2 teaspoons of superfine sugar.

COFFEE MORNINGS & AFTERNOON TEA

IN DAYS GONE BY, PEOPLE SEEMED TO HAVE THE TIME TO STOP FOR MORNING COFFEE OR AFTERNOON TEA. NOW, MOST OF US ARE TOO BUSY FOR MORE THAN A QUICK DRINK IN BETWEEN MAIN MEALS. SURELY IT IS TIME TO REVIVE THE CUSTOM, EVEN IF ONLY ON WEEKENDS, SO WITH FAMILY AND FRIENDS WE CAN ENJOY ONCE AGAIN THOSE DELICIOUS SCONES, MOIST CAKES, AND SANDWICHES.

Long-established teatime favorites like lemon sponge cake, shortbread, and crumpets from the Traditional Tea menu (page 174) should be served on delicate china (right).

COTTAGE

"How long does getting thin

RE-CREATE CHILDHOOD MEMORIES with pastel colored floral china, feather-light cakes with pretty icing, flowers, and, of course, many cups of restorative tea.

FLOWER VASE
Seasonal flowers in a cream-colored vase are most effective.

CRYSTALLIZED PETALS

Decorate iced cakes with edible sugared rose petals to match your tableware. Arrange them to resemble flowers or just scatter on the cake.

CHOCOLATE LEAVES

Turn an iced cake into a feast for the eyes by decorating it with an extravagant bow and leaves made using your favorite kind of chocolate.

1 Carefully remove petals from rose flowerheads and paint both sides of each one with lightly beaten egg white.

2 Use a tea strainer or small sieve to sprinkle both sides of each petal with superfine sugar before the egg white dries.

1 Melt chocolate until it is viscous but not runny. Paint it smoothly on one side of a firm, clean leaf.

2 Chill the chocolate until set, then gently peel the leaves off. Place among ribbons and bows as shown below.

FLORAL THEME
Arrange the sugared petals to resemble a flower. The green calyx is purely decorative and should not be eaten.

TRIMMINGS
Tie two lengths of silk ribbon in a sumptuous bow to make an enticing package.

take?' Pooh asked anxiously." A.A. MILNE 1882–1956

DISHES
Evoke the mood of bygone days with fine floral china.

CAKE
Pink and yellow petals on a sponge cake continue a cottage garden theme.

LACE TABLECLOTH
Delicately flowered lace works very well with traditional china.

GARLANDS

Fresh linen festooned with flowers and

SWAGS OF SUMMER FLOWERS are perfect for occasions when we wish to impress, perhaps at a garden party or christening tea.

FLORAL GARLAND
Make the garland by attaching bunches of wired flowers and leaves to lengths of light rope. Prepare small bunches of flowers and leaves first; you will need about 25 bunches per yard of garland. Allow yourself enough time – they cannot be hurried.

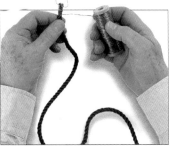

Bind to rope with turns of wire

1 Make a loop from which to hang the garland out of mossing wire, then securely tie this loop to the end of the rope.

2 Wire the first of your pre-prepared bunches of leaves and flowers to the rope so that it conceals the hanging loop.

NAPKIN FAN
Paper napkins fanned out on a plate are good for a crowd.

NEAT FINISH
If any wire shows, hide with foliage or cherries.

MIX & MATCH
Dress up the table still more with a silvery window box filled with flowers to match the garland.

graceful china

TEA URN
Combine practicality with great elegance: rent a decorative tea urn for large numbers of guests.

At least one stem must be strong and 3in (7cm) long to be wired onto rope

Twist wire around full length of stalks to secure

3 Bring the reel of wire back around, between the bunch and the rope. This will stop the bunch from coming undone.

4 Bind the rope and stems with wire. Add a second bunch just behind the first, and continue until the swag is filled.

LARGE BOW
Use fine tacks to hang the garland. Adorn any seams with a large bow.

MENUS
"Stands the Church clock at ten to three?

TRADITIONAL TEA

Teatime favorites that are wonderful served on the lawn in summer – or indoors in less clement weather. *Serves 12*

COFFEE, RUM & DATE CAKE
An exceedingly moist, syrup-soaked cake.

LEMON LAYER CAKE
Simplicity itself: a light cake redolent with piquant lemon.

CRUMPETS
Eat these warm, with melting butter, with butter and honey, or with butter and fruit preserves.

BUTTERY SHORTBREAD
A Scottish specialty, these rich tasty cookies are best when made at home.

DRINKS
Offer a choice of fragrant Orange Pekoe served without milk, or Earl Grey with or without milk.

PLANNING NOTES
Crumpets freeze particularly well, or they can be made up to one week ahead and kept in the refrigerator. Lightly toast to reheat, or serve straight from the griddle if cooking them after your guests have arrived. The cakes will keep in airtight tins for up to one week. *See pages 176–77 for recipes.*

FIRESIDE TEA

After a long afternoon walk, a warming tea by a fire is more than a pleasure. *Serves 6*

SCONES
These are an English classic served warm with cream and jam, or just butter.

UPSIDE-DOWN CAKE
Once sampled, this could become a firm favorite.

MAIDS OF HONOR
First made in the early eighteenth century in London, these filled tarts are justifiably still popular.

DRINKS
A choice of two teas: Lapsang Souchong served black, and a fine muscat-flavored Darjeeling with milk if preferred.

PLANNING NOTES
The upside-down cake will keep for up to one week in an airtight tin. Scones are best eaten soon after baking and while still warm, although they can be stored in an airtight tin and then warmed through in the oven when required. They also freeze well. Maids of Honor should be eaten the day they are made. *See pages 178–79 for recipes.*

And is there honey still for tea?" RUPERT BROOKE 1887–1915

COFFEE AT ELEVEN

Advise your guests to have a small breakfast
and no lunch date when you invite them for
morning coffee! *Serves 6*

CHOCOLATE BROWNIES
*This classic recipe is rich in chocolate without
being too sweet and cloying.*

BANANA & WALNUT LOAF
*A sweet banana bread that is popular with both adults
and children.*

SPICY APPLE CAKE
*The topping of this moist, open-textured cake flavored with
apple and spices is crunchy with sugar and nuts.*

DRINKS
*Jamaican Blue Mountain coffee made in a cafetiere
is the ideal choice for a special occasion.*

PLANNING NOTES
The banana and walnut loaf is good fresh, but delicious when
slightly stale (after a day) and lightly toasted. The brownies
and apple cake – best when fresh – can both be frozen, but
should then be eaten as soon as they have defrosted.
See pages 180–81 for recipes.

GARDEN PARTY TEA

An adaptable tea for large numbers on a special
occasion, perhaps at a christening. *Serves 12*

BRANDY SNAPS
*Crisp ginger and brandy cookies filled with
generous pipings of cream.*

NUTTY CHOCOLATE COOKIES
*No-flour cookies that are wickedly chocolatey, yet light
as a feather.*

FRUIT CAKE
*This moist and fruity cake is delicious and not
too heavy.*

DRINKS
*Earl Grey tea, with or without milk, and a homemade
fruit drink such as Apple Punch (see page 137 for recipe)
for children, make this a memorable tea party.*

PLANNING NOTES
Decorate the fruit cake with whole almonds, or cover in
marzipan and ice for a special occasion. Without icing, it lasts
for two weeks in an airtight tin. Store the cookies in tins, too,
for a maximum of one week. Brandy snaps keep well for a
few days in an airtight tin. The cream can be piped in up to
two hours before tea. *See pages 182–83 for recipes.*

TRADITIONAL TEA FOR 12

COFFEE, RUM & DATE CAKE

20 MINUTES · 40 MINUTES · 1 HOUR SOAKING

INGREDIENTS

SCANT 1 CUP (200ML) BOILING WATER
1½ CUPS (250G) DRIED DATES,
PITTED & COARSELY CHOPPED
2½ TBSP INSTANT COFFEE GRANULES
1 TSP BAKING SODA
1¼ CUPS (300G) SUGAR
½ CUP (100G) UNSALTED BUTTER, SOFTENED
4 LARGE EGGS: 2 WHOLE, 2 WHITE ONLY
1½ CUPS (175G) ALL-PURPOSE FLOUR, SIFTED
2 TSP BAKING POWDER, SIFTED
PINCH OF SALT
2 TSP VANILLA EXTRACT
3 TBSP DARK RUM
2LB (1KG) CONFECTIONERS' SUGAR
2 TBSP CORN SYRUP

COOK'S TIP

Dust the cake with confectioners' sugar at the end of Step 4 for a delicious, and faster, alternative.

1 Pour half of the boiling water over the dates. Stir in the coffee and baking soda. Let soak for 1 hour, then blend in a food processor.

2 Preheat oven to 350°F/180°C. Line an 8in (20cm) square or 9in (23cm) round cake pan with waxed paper, then grease it and lightly dust with flour. Cream together ½ cup (100g) of sugar and 5 tablespoons (75g) of butter until pale and fluffy. Lightly beat and add 2 whole eggs. Fold in the flour, baking powder, salt, and date mixture. Pour the batter into the pan and bake for 40 minutes.

3 To make the syrup, heat the vanilla and remaining water, sugar, and butter in a small saucepan and bring to a boil. Simmer for 15 minutes, then stir in the rum.

4 Leave the cake in its pan and pierce it all over with a skewer. Gradually pour over the syrup until it is absorbed into the cake. Cover the pan and let stand overnight before removing.

5 To make the roll-out icing, place the confectioners' sugar in a large mixing bowl and gradually mix in the 2 egg whites and corn syrup. Knead for about 10 minutes, adding a little more confectioners' sugar if the mixture is sticky. Roll out to fit the top and sides of the cake.

LEMON LAYER CAKE

25 MINUTES · 30 MINUTES · 1 HOUR SETTING

INGREDIENTS

2 CUPS (250G) SELF-RISING FLOUR, SIFTED
2 TSP BAKING POWDER, SIFTED
¾ CUP (375G) UNSALTED BUTTER, SOFTENED
1 CUP & 2 TBSP (250G) SUGAR
4 LARGE EGGS
1½ LEMONS, JUICE & GRATED ZEST
1LB (500G) CONFECTIONERS' SUGAR, SIFTED
2 TBSP BOILING WATER
4 TBSP LEMON MARMALADE
CRYSTALLIZED PETALS (SEE PAGE 170)
TO DECORATE

1 Preheat oven to 350°F/180°C. In a large mixing bowl, combine the flour, baking powder, 1 cup (250g) of the butter, the sugar, eggs, and lemon zest. Beat until well mixed.

2 Divide the mixture between two greased and lined 8in (20cm) loose-bottomed, round cake pans. Bake for about 30 minutes, until golden. Let the cakes cool for 2–3 minutes in their pans, then transfer to a wire rack to cool completely.

3 To make the icing, melt the remaining butter in a saucepan, remove from the heat, and beat in the confectioners' sugar, boiling water, and finally the lemon juice.

4 Sandwich the cakes together with lemon marmalade. Spread half of the icing over the top and sides of the cake. Let set for 1 hour. Beat the remaining icing and spread it in soft swirls over the top and sides. Decorate with Crystallized Petals.

CRUMPETS

☑ 30 MINUTES 🍳 40 MINUTES

▭ 2½ HOURS STANDING

INGREDIENTS

SCANT 1 CUP (200ML) MILK

1 TSP SUGAR

2 TSP INSTANT YEAST

2 TBSP VEGETABLE OIL

2¼ CUPS (550ML) TEPID WATER

2 CUPS (250G) BREAD FLOUR

2 CUPS (250G) ALL-PURPOSE FLOUR

2 TSP SALT

1 TSP BAKING SODA

1 In a saucepan, heat the milk and sugar until the sugar has dissolved. Remove the pan from the heat and let cool slightly. Add the yeast, let stand 10 minutes, then add the oil and 1½ cups (400ml) tepid water.

2 Sift both types of flour and salt into a mixing bowl. Gradually stir in the yeast mixture. Beat vigorously until smooth and elastic in consistency.

3 Cover the bowl with plastic wrap and a dish towel. Let stand in a warm place for 1½–2 hours until the mixture rises and the surface bubbles.

CRUMPETS

4 Dissolve the baking soda in the remaining water. Stir the batter so it collapses, add the baking soda mixture, cover, and leave for 30 minutes more.

5 Grease and flour three to five 3½in (8.5cm) plain ring molds. Place them on a griddle or frying pan over gentle heat. Three-quarters fill each ring with batter and cook for 8 minutes, until the surface sets and bubbles. Turn (still in molds) and cook for 4 minutes more, until golden.

6 Push the crumpets out of the rings onto a dish towel laid over a wire rack. Cover with another dish towel and keep warm in a low oven. Grease the rings again and cook the remaining batter. Serve warm with butter and honey or preserves.

BUTTERY SHORTBREAD

☑ 10 MINUTES 🍳 40 MINUTES

INGREDIENTS

2 CUPS (220G) ALL-PURPOSE FLOUR

¾ CUP (90G) RICE FLOUR

½ TSP SALT

6 TBSP (90G) SUGAR

¾ CUP (220G) UNSALTED BUTTER, IN PIECES

½ CUP (45G) HAZELNUTS, COARSELY CHOPPED & LIGHTLY TOASTED

CONFECTIONERS' SUGAR TO DUST

1 Preheat oven to 325°F/160°C. Sift both types of flour and salt into a mixing bowl. Stir in the sugar.

2 Add the butter to the sifted ingredients. Using your fingertips, rub the butter into the flour until well blended. Add the hazelnuts, then knead the dough gently. Press the dough into

a greased 9in (23cm) shallow square cake pan. Using a knife, indent halfway through the dough to mark into 24 fingers. Prick lightly with a fork.

3 Bake for about 40 minutes, until pale golden. Leave in the pan to cool. Cut into slices. Dust with confectioners' sugar before serving.

FIRESIDE TEA FOR 6

SCONES

⏱ 15 MINUTES 🍳 12 MINUTES

INGREDIENTS

2 CUPS (250G) ALL-PURPOSE FLOUR
1 TBSP BAKING POWDER
3 TBSP SUGAR
6 TBSP (90G) BUTTER, IN PIECES
¼ CUP (60G) DRIED APRICOTS, COARSELY
CHOPPED, OR GOLDEN RAISINS
1 LARGE EGG
6 TBSP (90ML) MILK
PRESERVES & MASCARPONE CHEESE TO SERVE

1 Preheat oven to 425°F/220°C. Sift the flour, baking powder, and sugar into a large bowl. Add the butter and, using fingertips or 2 knives, cut it in until the mixture is the consistency of fine bread crumbs. Stir in the apricots.

2 Beat together the egg and milk. Add gradually to the flour and butter mixture, reserving 2 tablespoons for glazing, until you have a soft dough that just comes away from the sides of the bowl.

3 Roll out the dough on a floured surface to about ¾ in (2cm) thick.

4 Cut out the dough using a 2in (5cm) round cutter. Place the scones on greased baking sheets and brush the tops with the reserved liquid. Bake for 10–12 minutes, until golden, then transfer to a wire rack.

5 Serve still slightly warm, halved, spread with apricot or other fruit preserve, and topped with mascarpone or fresh clotted cream.

COOK'S TIP
Scones can be frozen for up to 6 weeks, then defrosted and warmed in the oven.

UPSIDE-DOWN CAKE

⏱ 20 MINUTES 🍳 55 MINUTES

INGREDIENTS

¾ CUP (185G) BUTTER, SOFTENED
1 CUP (185G) SOFT BROWN SUGAR
½ LIME, GRATED ZEST & 1 TBSP JUICE
5 TBSP (75ML) RUM (OPTIONAL)
7 RINGS OF FRESH OR CANNED PINEAPPLE
½ CUP (125G) RAISINS
2 LARGE EGGS, LIGHTLY BEATEN
1½ CUPS (200G) SELF-RISING FLOUR
1 TSP BAKING POWDER
2 TBSP MILK

1 Preheat oven to 350°F/180°C. To make the topping, melt 4 tablespoons of the butter with ¼ cup (60g) of sugar and the lime juice in a small saucepan. Add 3 tablespoons of rum, if using. Pour the mixture into a greased 8in (20cm) round cake pan. Overlap the pineapple rings in the bottom of the pan and fill their centers and any gaps at the edges with half the raisins.

2 To make the cake, combine the remaining ingredients (except for the raisins) in a large bowl and beat for 2 minutes.

3 Fold in the remaining raisins. Spread the cake mixture over the pineapple slices and smooth the surface flat.

4 Bake for about 50 minutes, until risen and golden. Leave in its pan for 5 minutes, then turn out onto a wire rack to cool.

COOK'S TIPS
If you are omitting the rum, add an extra tablespoon of lime juice to the topping and 1–2 tablespoons of milk to the cake mixture. If you use fresh pineapple, cut it into ½ in (1cm) slices.

MAIDS OF HONOR

☑ 15 MINUTES ☐ 30 MINUTES ☐ 30 MINUTES CHILLING

INGREDIENTS

6OZ (175G) PUFF PASTRY (SEE PAGE 184)
SCANT 1 CUP (200ML) CRÈME FRAÎCHE
OR LIGHT SOUR CREAM
1 EGG, LIGHTLY BEATEN
1 TBSP UNSALTED BUTTER, MELTED
1 TBSP SUGAR
½ LEMON, ZEST ONLY
½ TSP GROUND NUTMEG

1 Roll out the pastry. Using a 3in (7.5cm) cutter, cut out 12 rounds and press into 12 muffin-tin holes. Lightly prick the pastry shells with a fork, then refrigerate for 30 minutes.

2 Preheat oven to 375°F/190°C. In a large bowl, mix together the remaining ingredients (except the nutmeg). Spoon the mixture into the chilled pastry shells, then sprinkle each of the tops with nutmeg.

3 Bake for 25–30 minutes until golden. Leave in muffin tin for 2 minutes before cooling on a wire rack.

COOK'S TIP

Make a tasty variation by adding half a teaspoon of ground cardamom seeds to the filling.

MAIDS OF
HONOR

UPSIDE-DOWN
CAKE

179

COFFEE AT ELEVEN FOR 6

CHOCOLATE BROWNIES

🥄 15 MINUTES 🍲 45 MINUTES

INGREDIENTS
3 TBSP ALL-PURPOSE FLOUR
1 TSP BAKING POWDER
PINCH OF SALT
2 TBSP COCOA POWDER
6OZ (175G) PLAIN DARK CHOCOLATE
5 TBSP (75G) UNSALTED BUTTER
3 LARGE EGGS
1 CUP (250G) SUGAR
1 TSP VANILLA EXTRACT
1 CUP (125G) PECANS, LIGHTLY
TOASTED & COARSELY CHOPPED
4 TBSP SOUR CREAM

1 Preheat oven to 350°F/180°C. Sift together the flour, baking powder, salt, and cocoa.

2 Break the chocolate into small pieces, then heat with the butter in a double boiler, a heatproof bowl over a saucepan of simmering water, or in a microwave, until just melted (do not overheat). Stir gently until smooth, but do not beat. Let cool slightly.

3 In a mixing bowl, beat the eggs, sugar, and vanilla until thick. Fold in the chocolate mixture, pecans, sour cream, and the sifted ingredients.

4 Turn the mixture into a lined 9in (23cm) square cake pan. Bake for about 45 minutes (the outside will be set, the center will be slightly soft). Cool in the pan for about 30 minutes, then transfer to a wire rack. When completely cool, cut into 12 squares.

COOK'S TIP
Walnuts, hazelnuts, or almonds can be used instead of pecans if you prefer.

BANANA & WALNUT LOAF

🥄 10–15 MINUTES 🍲 1 HOUR

INGREDIENTS
2 CUPS (250G) SELF-RISING FLOUR
½ TSP BAKING SODA
PINCH OF SALT
½ LIME, JUICE ONLY
3 MEDIUM BANANAS, MASHED
(ABOUT 1 CUP; 250G)
6 TBSP (90G) UNSALTED BUTTER, SOFTENED
½ CUP (125G) SUGAR
2 LARGE EGGS, LIGHTLY BEATEN
3 TBSP BUTTERMILK
½ CUP (60G) WALNUTS, COARSELY
CHOPPED

1 Preheat oven to 350°F/180°C. Sift together the flour, baking soda, and salt. Sprinkle the lime juice over the mashed banana.

2 In a large mixing bowl, cream together the butter and sugar until pale and fluffy, then add the beaten eggs and banana and lime. Finally, gently fold in the sifted ingredients alternately with the chopped walnuts and buttermilk, until all the ingredients are thoroughly combined.

3 Turn the mixture into a greased 9 x 5in (23 x 13cm) loaf pan. Bake for 1 hour, until the loaf has risen and is golden. Leave the loaf in its pan for 5 minutes, then cool on a wire rack. Serve with unsalted butter.

COOK'S TIP
You can substitute chopped pecans, hazelnuts, or almonds for the walnuts.

SPICY APPLE
CAKE

BANANA &
WALNUT LOAF

SPICY APPLE CAKE

20 MINUTES   55 MINUTES

INGREDIENTS

2 CUPS (475G) SUGAR
½ CUP (125G) UNSALTED BUTTER, MELTED
1 CUP (100G) PECANS, COARSELY CHOPPED
1 TSP GROUND CLOVES
1¼ LB (625G) GREEN COOKING APPLES
5 TBSP (75ML) WATER
3 LARGE EGGS
2 TSP VANILLA EXTRACT
1 CUP (275G) ALL-PURPOSE FLOUR, SIFTED
2 TSP BAKING POWDER, SIFTED
1 TSP GROUND CINNAMON
PINCH OF SALT
5 CUPS (75G) DRIED APPLE OR DRIED PEAR,
COARSELY CHOPPED

1 Preheat oven to 375°F/190°C. First, prepare the topping. Combine ⅔ cup (150g) of the sugar, 5 tablespoons (75g) of the butter, the pecans, and ½ teaspoon ground cloves. Set aside.

2 Next, make the apple purée: peel, core, and cut the cooking apples into chunks. Place in a saucepan with the water and cook, covered, for 8 minutes, until soft. Work in a blender to make a purée.

3 In a large mixing bowl, beat the eggs and vanilla until thickened, then add the remaining sugar. Fold in the flour, baking powder, cinnamon, salt, and remaining cloves, then the apple purée, remaining butter, and dried apple.

4 Pour the mixture into a lined and greased 9in (23cm) springform cake pan. Bake for 15 minutes, then remove from the oven and spoon over the topping. Return the cake to the oven and bake for 25–30 minutes more. Leave in its pan until completely cool.

COOK'S TIP
If time is short, use 1 cup (250ml) store-bought applesauce instead of making the purée (Step 2).

GARDEN PARTY TEA FOR 12

BRANDY SNAPS
🥄 10 MINUTES 🍲 16 MINUTES

INGREDIENTS
4 TBSP UNSALTED BUTTER
4 TBSP SUGAR
4 TBSP LIGHT CORN SYRUP
1 TBSP BRANDY (OPTIONAL)
4 TBSP ALL-PURPOSE FLOUR, SIFTED
1 TSP GROUND GINGER
BRANDIED CREAM (SEE PAGE 163, STEP 5)

1 Preheat oven to 350°F/180°C. In a small saucepan over gentle heat, combine the butter, sugar, corn syrup, and brandy, if using, until the butter has melted and the sugar dissolved. Remove from the heat and stir in the flour and ginger. Return to very low heat to keep warm.

2 Line 2 baking sheets with waxed paper. Drop 3 teaspoons of mixture onto each sheet, about 5in (12cm) apart, spreading in a circular motion to make 4in (10cm) rounds.

3 Bake for 7–8 minutes, until golden. Let cool for 1 minute, then roll each cookie around the oiled handle of a wooden spoon. If the cookies become too hard to roll, return to the oven briefly to soften. Remove and place on a wire rack to cool. Continue to bake and roll batches of cookies until all the mixture is used.

4 Prepare the Brandied Cream. Pipe the cream into each end of the brandy snap cylinders.

COOK'S TIP
This mixture will also make 6 Ginger Baskets. Bake 6 large cookies in the same way, then drape each one over an upside-down teacup to form a fluted bowl. When cold, remove the cup.

NUTTY CHOCOLATE COOKIES
🥄 25 MINUTES 🍲 10 MINUTES

INGREDIENTS
7OZ (200G) DARK CHOCOLATE
4 LARGE EGGS, WHITES ONLY
1 CUP (200G) SUGAR
2 TSP VANILLA EXTRACT
1 TSP VINEGAR
2 CUPS (200G) PECAN NUTS, COARSELY CHOPPED & LIGHTLY TOASTED

1 Preheat oven to 375°F/190°C. Break the chocolate into small pieces, then heat in a double boiler, a heatproof bowl over a saucepan of simmering water, or in a microwave. Stir the chocolate gently as it melts, but do not beat. Let cool slightly.

2 In a large bowl, whisk the egg whites until they form soft peaks. Add the sugar, a little at a time, whisking after each addition, until the peaks hold firm.

3 Fold in the vanilla and vinegar, then the melted chocolate and pecans.

4 Line 2 baking sheets with waxed paper and drop 12 large tablespoons of mixture onto each sheet, about 3in (7cm) apart, slightly smoothing down the mixture to make 2½in (6cm) disks.

5 Bake for 10 minutes (they should be slightly sticky). Leave on the baking sheet for 1 minute, then transfer to a wire rack to cool.

COOK'S TIPS
These cookies keep well for at least 1 week in an airtight container. Walnuts, almonds, or hazelnuts could be used instead of pecans.

FRUIT CAKE

10 MINUTES ☕ 1½ HOURS 🍰 2 HOURS COOLING

INGREDIENTS
½ CUP (125G) UNSALTED BUTTER
¾ CUP (175G) SUGAR
2 CUPS (375G) RAISINS
1¼ CUPS (250G) GOLDEN RAISINS
4 EARL GREY TEA BAGS
1 CUP (250ML) WATER
2 LIMES, JUICE & GRATED ZEST
1 TSP BAKING SODA
1 CUP (125G) ALL-PURPOSE FLOUR
1 CUP (125G) SELF-RISING FLOUR
1 TSP GROUND CLOVES
1 TSP GROUND NUTMEG
PINCH OF SALT
2 LARGE EGGS, LIGHTLY BEATEN
½ CUP (60G) WHOLE SHELLED ALMONDS

1 In a saucepan, heat the butter, sugar, raisins, golden raisins, tea bags, water, lime juice and zest, and baking soda. Bring to a boil, then simmer for 5 minutes. Squeeze the tea bags gently into the liquid to release their flavor.

2 Let the mixture cool for about 2 hours. Discard the tea bags.

3 Preheat oven to 350°F/180°C. In a large mixing bowl, sift together both types of flour, the cloves, nutmeg, and salt. Add the eggs and then the fruit mixture. Mix well.

4 Line and grease an 8in (20cm) round cake pan. Spoon in the cake mixture. Arrange the almonds over the top of the cake.

5 Bake for about 1¼–1½ hours, until golden. Leave the cake in its pan for 10 minutes, then transfer to a wire rack to cool.

COOK'S TIP
This cake will keep extremely well in an airtight tin for up to 3 weeks.

NUTTY
CHOCOLATE
COOKIES

FRUIT CAKE

BASIC RECIPES

PASTRY

PUFF PASTRY

INGREDIENTS FOR 1½ LB (750G)
3 CUPS (375G) ALL-PURPOSE FLOUR, SIFTED
PINCH OF SALT
1½ CUPS (375G) BUTTER, WELL CHILLED,
IN PIECES
10 TBSP (150ML) ICE WATER
3 TSP LEMON JUICE

Place the flour, salt, and butter in a large mixing bowl. Using a knife, toss the butter pieces in the flour until they are coated. Mix the water with the lemon juice and add to the bowl, using the knife to mix in the liquid and keeping the butter in pieces as long as possible.

When the mix just binds together, transfer to a floured surface and roll into a rectangle about 6 x 14in (15 x 35cm). Fold the top third of the rectangle down, then the bottom third up over it. Press the edges together to seal. Wrap in a plastic bag or plastic wrap and refrigerate for 15 minutes. Remove from the refrigerator, place on a floured surface, and with the unfolded edges at the top and bottom, roll into a rectangle, fold and seal as before, and refrigerate for 15 minutes.

Repeat this process twice more, then refrigerate for 30 minutes before using.

SHORTCRUST PASTRY

INGREDIENTS FOR 1LB (500G)
2½ CUPS (300G) ALL-PURPOSE FLOUR, SIFTED
PINCH OF SALT
5 TBSP (75G) BUTTER, IN PIECES
5 TBSP (75G) LARD OR SHORTENING,
IN PIECES
2 TSP ICE WATER

Place the flour, salt, butter, and lard in a food processor and work until the mixture is the consistency of bread crumbs.

Add the water and process until the mixture just holds together, adding a little more water if necessary.

Gather the mixture into a soft ball and wrap in a plastic bag or plastic wrap. Refrigerate for at least 30 minutes before using.

SWEET SHORTCRUST PASTRY

INGREDIENTS FOR 1LB (500G)
2 CUPS (250G) ALL-PURPOSE FLOUR, SIFTED
PINCH OF SALT
¼ CUP (60G) SUGAR
1¼ CUPS (150G) UNSALTED BUTTER, IN PIECES
2 LARGE EGGS, YOLKS ONLY, LIGHTLY BEATEN

Place the flour, salt, sugar, and butter in a food processor and work until the mixture is the consistency of bread crumbs.

Add the egg yolks and process briefly until the mixture just holds together.

Wrap in a plastic bag or wrap and refrigerate for 1 hour before using.

COOK'S PASTRY TIPS

When making pastry without a food processor, cut the butter into the dry ingredients using a knife, or mix them together with your fingertips. When the mixture is the consistency of bread crumbs, gradually cut in or mix in the egg yolks.

Use chilled water to make pastry dough and add just enough to make the dough bind. It is important to add the liquid carefully; too much will make the cooked pastry tough, and too little will produce crumbly baked pastry.

If you have time, let the pastry rest in the refrigerator for more than 30 minutes: this helps to prevent it from shrinking when it is baked.

When baking, brush the base of the case with about 2 tablespoons lightly beaten egg yolk after removing the beans from the case, before returning the pastry to the oven: this prevents it from becoming soggy when the filling is added.

Pastry can be frozen for up to 6 weeks or kept in the refrigerator for 3 days.

STOCKS

FOR 3 QUARTS (3 LITERS)

VEGETABLE STOCK

3 TBSP OLIVE OIL
4 ONIONS, FINELY CHOPPED
4 CELERY STICKS, CHOPPED
4 CARROTS, CHOPPED
2 BAY LEAVES
1 TBSP FRESH OREGANO, FINELY CHOPPED
½ TSP GROUND GINGER
2 TSP SALT
3 QUARTS (3 LITERS) WATER

Heat the oil in a large saucepan, add the onions, celery, and carrots, and cook over moderate heat for 6 minutes. Add the remaining ingredients, bring to a boil, and simmer for 1½ hours. Strain the stock through a fine sieve and let cool. Freeze (for up to 6 weeks) or refrigerate until needed.

FISH STOCK

1 LB (500G) RAW SHRIMP, SHELLS ON
8 ANCHOVY FILLETS
ANY OTHER FISH BONES & SKIN (OPTIONAL)
3 QUARTS (3 LITERS) WATER
3 ONIONS, FINELY CHOPPED
1 BAY LEAF
1 LEMON, JUICE ONLY
SALT TO TASTE

Crush the shrimp in their shells and place them with all the remaining ingredients (except the salt) in a large saucepan. Bring to a boil, then simmer, covered, for 1½ hours, skimming occasionally to remove any scum. Remove from the heat and add salt to taste. Strain through a fine sieve and let cool. Freeze (for up to 6 weeks) or refrigerate until needed.

CHICKEN STOCK

2 CHICKEN CARCASSES
3 QUARTS (3 LITERS) WATER
3 ONIONS, FINELY CHOPPED
2 TSP GROUND BLACK PEPPER
4 GARLIC CLOVES, CRUSHED
1 BAY LEAF
2 TSP FRESH THYME, FINELY CHOPPED

Place all the ingredients in a saucepan and bring to a boil. Simmer, covered, for 2½ hours, skimming occasionally to remove any scum. Strain through a fine sieve, and let cool. Freeze (for up to 6 weeks) or refrigerate until needed.

SALAD DRESSINGS

FOR 12 SERVINGS

WALNUT OR HAZELNUT

3 TSP VINEGAR
4 TSP LEMON JUICE
PINCH SALT, PEPPER & SUGAR
4 TBSP WALNUT OR HAZELNUT OIL
6 TBSP (90ML) VEGETABLE OIL

Whisk the vinegar and lemon juice with the salt, pepper, and sugar until well mixed. Drizzle in the oils slowly, beating all the time to form an emulsion. The dressing will keep in the refrigerator, covered, for up to 1 week.

VINAIGRETTE

4 TSP VINEGAR
4 TSP DIJON MUSTARD
PINCH SALT & PEPPER
10 TBSP (150ML) OLIVE OIL

Whisk the vinegar, mustard, and seasoning until well mixed. Slowly drizzle in the olive oil, beating all the time until it forms a thick, creamy sauce. The dressing will keep in the refrigerator, covered, for up to 1 week.

SHARP SWEET

3 LIMES, JUICE & GRATED ZEST
½ FRESH GREEN CHILI
2 GARLIC CLOVES, CRUSHED
PINCH SALT & PEPPER
3 TBSP WATER
3 TSP SUGAR

Seed and finely chop the chili. Whisk all the ingredients together until well mixed. The dressing will keep in the refrigerator, covered, for up to 1 week. This dressing is excellent served with salads including exotic fruits such as mango and papaya.

ACCOMPANIMENTS
FOR 12 SERVINGS

FOCACCIA

1 ENVELOPE INSTANT YEAST
2 TSP SALT
2LB (1KG) BREAD FLOUR
½ CUP (120G) OLIVE OIL
1½ CUPS (450ML) LUKEWARM WATER
1 TBSP SEA SALT
2 TBSP FRESH SAGE, FINELY CHOPPED

Mix the yeast, salt, half of the flour, 3 tablespoons of the olive oil, and about half of the water in a large bowl. Gradually work in the remaining flour and as much water as it takes to make a soft but not sticky dough.

Knead the dough on a floured surface for 15 minutes, until it is smooth and elastic. Place the dough in a large, oiled plastic bag and let rise at warm room temperature for 1½–2 hours.

Punch the risen dough down and form it into a flat rectangle about ½ in (1cm) thick. Place it on a lightly oiled baking sheet, cover with plastic, and let it rise again for 45 minutes. Preheat oven to 450°F/230°C.

After the second rising, make dents with your fingertips all over the top of the dough and brush on a mixture of the remaining olive oil whisked with 2 tablespoons of lukewarm water. (This mixture will run into the holes made by your fingers.) Sprinkle with the sea salt and sage, and bake for 20–25 minutes.

NEW POTATO SALAD

3LB (1.5 KG) SMALL NEW POTATOES
1 TBSP RED WINE VINEGAR
2 TBSP WHOLE-GRAIN MUSTARD
2 TBSP FRESH DILL, FINELY CHOPPED
SALT & PEPPER TO TASTE
7 TBSP (105ML) OLIVE OIL
1 GARLIC CLOVE, HALVED

Cook the potatoes in a large saucepan of boiling salted water until just cooked, but not soft. The cooking time will depend on the variety of potato you use. Drain immediately, and as soon as you can handle the potatoes cut them into medium-thick slices.

In a small bowl, mix the vinegar, mustard, dill, and seasoning very well, then drizzle in the oil, beating all the time until you have an emulsion. Rub a serving dish with the cut edges of the garlic, add the warm potatoes, and gently toss them in the dressing.

HERBY POTATOES

3 TBSP OLIVE OIL
3LB (1.5KG) NEW POTATOES, CUT INTO HALVES
4 GARLIC CLOVES, CRUSHED
2 TBSP EACH FRESH THYME & FRESH MARJORAM, FINELY CHOPPED
2 BAY LEAVES, TORN
SALT TO TASTE
VEGETABLE STOCK (SEE PAGE 185)

Heat the oil in a large saucepan, add the potatoes and garlic, and sauté until they just begin to brown. Add the thyme, marjoram, bay leaves, salt, and enough vegetable stock to come just over halfway up the potatoes. Boil gently, uncovered, for 30 minutes, until little liquid remains.

Remove from the heat and chop the potatoes, incorporating the remaining liquid in the saucepan, until they are the consistency of coarse mashed potato.

COOK'S TIPS
You may need to adjust the seasoning once you have chopped the potatoes. Halve the recipe to serve 6 people, or make 2 batches if you are cooking for larger numbers.

BAY ROAST POTATOES

12 BAKING POTATOES, SCRUBBED
1 TBSP OLIVE OIL
1 TSP SALT
12 BAY LEAVES, CUT IN HALF CROSSWISE

Preheat oven to 400°F/200°C. Make two deep cuts into each potato, about three-quarters of the way down. Rub each potato with oil, then slip the bay-leaf halves into the cuts.

Place on a baking sheet, sprinkle salt onto the potatoes, and bake for about 1 hour, or until brown and cooked through (the cooking time may vary depending on the size of the potatoes, so test them with a skewer).

COOK'S TIP
Red-skinned potatoes are excellent when cooked this way.

ROAST SHALLOTS

36 SHALLOTS, PEELED
4 TBSP BUTTER
2 TSP SUGAR

Place the shallots, butter, and sugar in a heavy frying pan with a lid. Cook over moderate heat, shaking occasionally until the shallots begin to brown. Turn the heat down to the lowest setting and cook, covered, for 30 minutes, until the shallots are nutty brown and cooked through.

BRAISED ENDIVE

½ CUP (125G) BUTTER
12 HEADS OF BELGIAN ENDIVE, HALVED
2 LEMONS, JUICE & GRATED ZEST

Preheat oven to 375°F/180°C. Heat the butter in a frying pan, add the endive, and lightly brown all over. Remove from heat and arrange in a single layer in a shallow baking dish with a lid, using two dishes if necessary. Pour over the lemon juice and sprinkle with the zest.

Cover the dish and bake for 1 hour, remove lid, and continue to cook for 20 minutes, or until endive is brown and caramelized. Serve two halves each.

CELERIAC RÉMOULADE

1 LARGE CELERIAC, PEELED
1 LEMON, JUICE & GRATED ZEST
6 TBSP (90ML) MAYONNAISE (SEE PAGE 147)
3 TBSP DIJON MUSTARD
¼ TSP GROUND CHILI POWDER
SALT TO TASTE

Coarsely grate the celeriac, then toss immediately in the lemon juice. Add the remaining ingredients and stir briskly to ensure that the celeriac is completely coated.

COOK'S TIP
This recipe is also delicious made with half celeriac, half grated fresh carrot. Double or halve the quantities proportionately.

COUSCOUS

2 TBSP SESAME OIL
4 TSP GROUND CORIANDER
4 TSP GROUND TURMERIC
4 CUPS (1 LITER) WATER
½ CUP (125G) GOLDEN RAISINS
SALT TO TASTE
4 CUPS (750G) COUSCOUS
4 TBSP BUTTER

Heat the oil, coriander, and turmeric in a saucepan and cook until the spices begin to brown. Add the water, golden raisins, and salt, and bring to a boil.

Remove from the heat and add the couscous in a steady stream, stirring all the time. Cover and let stand for 10 minutes. Add the butter and cook over low heat for 5 minutes, stirring continuously. It can be kept warm in a low oven for up to 2 hours, covered tightly. Fluff with a fork before serving.

SAFFRON RICE

4 CUPS (750G) BASMATI RICE
2 TBSP BUTTER
1 TBSP OLIVE OIL
3 GARLIC CLOVES, SKINS LEFT ON, CRUSHED UNDER THE FLAT OF A KNIFE
2⅔ CUPS (660ML) CHICKEN STOCK (SEE PAGE 185) OR WATER
1 TSP SAFFRON THREADS, CRUSHED
3 TSP SALT

Wash the rice in a sieve under running water until the water runs clear.

Heat the butter, oil, and garlic in a large saucepan over medium heat. When the butter has melted, add the rice and stir until coated. Add the chicken stock, saffron, and salt, stir well, and bring to a boil. Turn the heat to low and cook, covered, for 8 minutes. Remove from the heat, discard the garlic, and let stand for 3 minutes with the lid on before serving.

RECIPE LIST

BREAKFASTS

Bubble & Squeak 42
Coeur à la Crème & Passion Fruit 40
Cranberry Muffins 37
Creamy Scrambled Eggs 43
Golden Corn & Green Pea Pancakes 39
Herbed Tomatoes 43
Mango & Papaya 36
Orange & Lime Marmalade 43
Pernod Pears in Grapefruit Juice 38
Prosciutto, Shrimp & Apples 38
Provençal Pipérade 37
Rich Lemon Curd 41
Spicy Kedgeree 41

BREADS & CAKES

Banana & Walnut Loaf 180
Brandy Snaps 182
Buttery Shortbread 177
Chocolate Birthday Cake 115
Chocolate Brownies 180
Coffee, Rum & Date Cake 176
Crumpets 177
Focaccia 186
Fruit Cake 183
Homemade Oat Cookies 120
Lemon Layer Cake 176
Maids of Honor 179
Nutty Chocolate Cookies 182
Raisin & Oregano Soda Bread 160
Scones 178
Spicy Apple Cake 181
Upside-Down Cake 178

APPETIZERS

Arugula Soup 88
Asparagus & Ham Fettuccine 102
Brie & Lentil Salad 90
Crab Tartlets with Leek Purée 82
Duck & Arugula Salad 166
Fig & Feta Salad 54

Herb Omelet with Caviar 84
Italian Cabbage Soup 100
Marinated Salmon 118
Peppered Scallops 86
Potato & Bacon Salad 58
Roast Tomato Soup 92
Salad Niçoise 163
Seared Goat Cheese & Tapenade 150
Seared Pears & Prosciutto 80
Shrimp in Hard Cider 94
Shrimp, Leek & Saffron Soup 98
Shrimp Soup 56
Wild Mushroom Ragoût 96

MAIN COURSES

Blue Cheese Soufflés 92
Broccoli & Pine Nut Fettuccine 116
Cassoulet 114
Charred Squid 146
Chicken Crepe Stack 118
Crispy Chicken Livers 148
Duck with Kumquats 83
Fennel & Cheese Tart 167
Fish Cakes with Herb Sauce 63
Flemish-Style Beef 98
Fresh Sautéed Sardines 54
Ginger & Garlic Chicken 152
Herbed Country Pâté 161
Lamb Tagine with Couscous 87
Lobster with Roast Figs 84
Mixed Mushroom Kebabs 151
Oriental Bundles with Spicy Sauce 57
Parslied Ham 161
Peppered Lamb 58
Pheasant & Apples with Calvados 97
Pissaladière 162
Pork with Tuna Sauce 121
Red Mullet with Fennel & Orange 147
Scallops with Chard 80
Seared Beef with Thai Sauce 153
Shrimp & Mushroom Papardelle 116
Spicy Chicken with Papaya Salad 164

Spicy Lamb Kebabs 165
Spicy Pork Roast 100
Tarragon Chicken 88
Tea-Smoked Tuna 148
Trout with Gooseberry Sauce 91
Tuna Steaks with Rhubarb 94
Vegetable & Nut Kebabs 102

DESSERTS

Aromatic Fruit Salad 55
Blueberry Tart 61
Chocolate & Coffee Cheesecake 97
Chocolate Tart 81
Coconut & Saffron Ice Cream 87
Coffee & Amaretto Ice Cream 117
Coffee Truffle Puddings 93
Fresh Fruit Savarin 119
Ginger Sorbet 57
Indian Milk Pudding 165
Lime & Mint Mold 89
Mango Syllabub & Almond Cookies 95
Miraculous Blackberry Cake 101
Orange & Grapefruit Sorbets 85
Peppered Pineapple 147
Polenta Cake 167
Quince Tart Tatin 163
Roasted Plantains with Rum Sauce 149
Spiced Quinces & Earl Grey Sorbet 103
Steamed Cranberry Pudding 99
Strawberry Tart 91
Summer Fruits with Crème Fraîche 83
West Indian Punch Gelatin 121
Winter Compote & Prune Ice Cream 59

COCKTAIL FOOD

Cocktail Kebabs 130
Crostini 132
Fruits with Prosciutto 131
Phyllo Bundles 131
Sushi 133

INDEX

ACKNOWLEDGMENTS

AUTHOR'S ACKNOWLEDGMENTS

Working on this book has been a joy. Firstly, I would like to thank photographers Martin Brigdale and Stephen Hayward for their magnificent photography: Martin for the food, and Stephen for the flowers and the table settings.

Thank you also to the wonderful DK team of editor Lesley (munch) Malkin and art editor Murdo (munch, munch) Culver.

Thanks, too, to Helen Trent, who, with her magic eye (and the odd few sneezes), located so much beautiful china, glass, cutlery, and table linen. Janey Suthering and Janice Murfitt did the most wonderful job of preparing all the food for the photographic sessions – eating the spoils at lunchtime was a very special bonus!

Dennis, Lee, and David at John Austin, New Covent Garden Market, were the usual invaluable aids, especially at finding so many out-of-season flowers. My appreciation as well to Terracottas, also of New Covent Garden, for the loan of special containers. Finally, and most importantly, I would like to thank Rodney "Cocktails" Engen for all his constructive help with the book and also, together with a big heap of my friends, for being a guinea pig for a year while I was making and testing all the recipes.

PUBLISHER'S ACKNOWLEDGMENTS

Thank you to Anna Cheifetz and Polly Boyd for editorial help, particularly on the recipes, and also to Richard Hammond and Clare Double. For additional design help, thanks to Pauline Clarke, Sharon Moore, and Deborah Myatt. We would also like to thank Emma Patmore for testing the recipes, with the exception of those in the Breakfast & Brunch, Lunch, and Coffee Mornings & Afternoon Tea chapters; thank you to Jill Eggleton, who tested these. Thanks also to Mark Bracey for DTP guidance, and to Hilary Bird for compiling the index.

PICTURE CREDITS

All food photography by Martin Brigdale, and all other photography by Stephen Hayward, with the exception of:

Alan Williams 29 tc; Dave King 41 tr, 60 bl, 91 br, 114 tr, 145 tl; David Murray 58 cl, 96 tr, 114 bl; Ian O'Leary 83 cl, 145 tc, 175 tc; Jacqui Hurst 77 tc; Joe Cornish 49 tr; John Glover 175 tr; Martin Norris 56 tr; Matthew Ward 79 tl; Max Alexander 145 tr; Philip Dowell 147 br, 153 br, 166 tr, 182 cl; Steven Wooster 71 tc, 77 tr, 79 tr, 159 tr, 171 tc.

t=top, c=center, b=bottom, r=right, l=left

THE FOLLOWING KINDLY LOANED PROPS FOR PHOTOGRAPHY

DIVERTIMENTI
44 Fulham Road
London SW3 6HH

For serving dishes, pasta bowls, and plates used on pages: 22–3, 27, 28–9, 139, and 140–41.

THOMAS GOODE & CO. (LONDON) LTD.
19 South Audley Street
London W1Y 6BN

For serving dishes, plates, cutlery, glasses, and place mats used on pages: 63, 64–5, 105, and 106–7.

VILLEROY & BOCH
267 Merton Road
London SW19 5JS

For glasses, cutlery, and plates used on pages: 110–11.